"Charles Kimball, one of our best teachers, pow_____ what the Muslim faith truly is, despite how it is n_____ He teaches us that the hard work of understanding different faiths is a way to genuinely find peace and justice in the world. *Truth over Fear* gives me hope for how our different faith traditions, each being what they distinctly are, can together help transform the world instead of helping tear it apart. I can think of no better book for those seeking a practical and deeply empathetic treatment of interfaith understanding and cooperation."

—**Jim Wallis**, *New York Times* bestselling author of *America's Original Sin: Racism, White Privilege, and the Bridge to a New America*, President of Sojourners, and Editor-in-Chief of *Sojourners* magazine

"This slim book is so full of vital information, lived experience, and practical guidance that it should weigh pounds instead of ounces—but above all else, it is filled with hope. I finished the last page with a great swell of gratitude to Charles Kimball for showing me how Christians and Muslims of good faith can work together for the common good, living up to the highest teachings of their traditions at the same time. Don't buy one copy—buy a dozen, since you will want to give this book to everyone you know."

—**Barbara Brown Taylor**, author of *Holy Envy: Finding God in the Faith of Others*

"Charles Kimball has written an important book: a text that is all at once a primer on Islam, a practical guide for peacemakers, and an inspirational vision for a world based on interfaith cooperation. Read this book and join the movement to make faith a bridge of cooperation rather than a barrier of division."

—**Dr. Eboo Patel**, Founder and President of Interfaith Youth Core, author of *Acts of Faith: The Story of an American Muslim, the Struggle for the Soul of a Generation* and *Out of Many Faiths: Religious Diversity and the American Promise*

"*Truth over Fear: Combating the Lies about Islam* is an important, engaging, and accessible book, a "must read" for our times when Islamophobia has become normalized. Charles Kimball, prominent Islamic studies scholar and a leader in Christian-Muslim relations nationally and internationally, enables a broad readership to understand and overcome the lies that have fueled Islamophobia: anti-Muslim bias, discrimination, and the hate crimes that have affected the lives and civil liberties of Muslims in the United States, Europe, China, Myanmar, New Zealand and beyond."

—**John L. Esposito**, Founding Director of the Alwaleed Center for Muslim-Christian Understanding, Georgetown University, and author of *The Future of Islam*

"Drawing on his academic expertise as well as on his long-standing, on-the-ground experience in promoting Muslim-Christian relations in the Middle East, Kimball offers Christians both an antidote to Islamophobia and practical guidelines for engaging and working with their Muslim neighbors. Clearly written, this is a book that both instructs and inspires. Highly recommended for both parish discussion groups and undergraduate classrooms."
—**Paul F. Knitter,** Paul Tillich Professor Emeritus of Theology and World Religions, Union Theological Seminary

"As a close colleague and an interfaith partner with Charles Kimball, I have witnessed firsthand his sincerity and dedication to peace. This book encapsulates interfaith cooperation that is so urgently needed today by presenting a pragmatic approach to interfaith relations and peace building. Read this book with an open heart and mind and it will not only transform you to be an advocate for healthy interfaith relationships, but it will also make you a partner for peace."
—**Dr. Imad S. Enchassi,** Senior Imam, Islamic Society of Greater Oklahoma City; Mercy Chair of Islamic Studies and Muslim Chaplain, Oklahoma City University

"Charles Kimball's remarkable new book captures the rich fruits of his forty years in Christian ministry, interfaith activism, university teaching, and global ecumenical outreach. He explains all the critical issues in Christian-Muslim relations, which he has lived through and worked on for decades. Clearly and concisely, he offers vital historical and theological background along with practical suggestions for how individuals and communities can break down the walls of ignorance, fear, and mistrust that plague us today. If you are concerned, confused, or just curious about tensions between Christians and Muslims, this is the place to start walking toward understanding and peace."
—**Rami G. Khouri,** syndicated columnist, Agence Global Syndicate, USA; Nonresident Senior Fellow at the Kennedy School, Harvard University; Senior Public Policy Fellow, Journalist-in-Residence, and Adjunct Professor of journalism, American University of Beirut

"I highly recommend Charles Kimball's *Truth over Fear* as a must-read for anyone seeking to better understand Islam and the relationships among different faith traditions in the twenty-first century. This insightful and accessible book covers the basic tenets of Islam while also calling for a faithful response and peaceful coexistence. Kimball's expertise and years of experience in ministry and international religious dialogue provide key insights for anyone desiring to combat 'the lies about Islam' and to live in peace and harmony with their Muslim neighbors."
—**Rev. Dr. Mae Elise Cannon,** Executive Director of Churches for Middle East Peace; editor of *A Land Full of God: Christian Perspectives on the Holy Land*; author of *Social Justice Handbook: Small Steps for a Better World* and *Just Spirituality: How Faith Practices Fuel Social Action*

"In *Truth over Fear*, Charles Kimball distills several decades of immersion experience in the Christian faith, deep study of Islam, and direct engagement in Muslim-Christian relations in a variety of contexts to give us perhaps the most lucid, comprehensive, and reliable account of Islam, and the past, present, and the possible future relationship between Christians and Muslims. It is brutally honest about the truth and lies that have beset this relationship over the centuries. By posing searching questions for discussion at the end of each chapter, Kimball invites all of us to reflect in depth about the many facets of this relationship that will have far-reaching consequences to our life as a human community in the decades ahead. I hope that clergy, study groups, and those engaged in teaching or facilitating Muslim-Christian relations will use and promote this volume as an invaluable resource for understanding and fostering Muslim-Christian relations today."

—**Rev. Dr. S. Wesley Ariarajah,** Professor Emeritus of Ecumenical Theology at the Drew University School of Theology and former Director of the Interfaith Dialogue Program of the World Council of Churches; author of *The Bible and People of Other Faiths, Not without My Neighbour,* and *Strangers or Co-Pilgrims? The Impact of Interfaith Dialogue on Christian Faith and Practice*

"Each week a worshiper comes to me wanting help in sorting through love-based information versus fear-based disinformation about Islam. I'm so eager to have multiple copies of Charles Kimball's enlightening resource to hand them. Kimball's work makes our world and history more hopeful because he genuinely knows what interreligious community looks like."

—**Ed Bacon,** Rector Emeritus, All Saints Church, Pasadena; Interim Rector, St. Luke's Episcopal Church, Atlanta; author, *8 Habits of Love: Open Your Heart, Open Your Mind*

"*Truth over Fear* goes to the top of my list of resources for Christians wanting to understand the faith of their Islamic neighbors and engage in authentic, respectful, informed dialogue that does not sacrifice the distinctiveness of either faith but acknowledges important common ground for building communities of peace. Kimball articulately counters the myths of the clash of cultures and Islam as a monolithic force to be feared. The chapter on the missionary mandate and interfaith dialogue will be very helpful to Christians who wrestle with whether evangelism or dialogue is their most faithful response to people of other faiths."

—**Rev. Dr. A. Roy Medley,** General Secretary Emeritus, American Baptist Churches; Cofounder of the North American Baptist-Muslim Dialogue; Chairperson of the Commission on Interfaith Relations of the Baptist World Alliance

"If ever we needed this book, we need it now. If ever we needed a competent, committed Christian to write it, we have found him in Charles Kimball. And if you are a Christian, here is both what you need to know and what you need to do to bring about a more peaceful world. I wish every adult Sunday school class in America would study it."

—**Dr. Walter B. Shurden,** Minister at Large, Mercer University

"Honesty demands that we admit how little most of us know about the world's second-largest religion or how often that ignorance has enabled the forces of hatred and division. We need to do more than just feel regret. We need to study, to learn, and to bear witness to the truth. Charles Kimball has written an invaluable resource and explained through personal experience why the stakes are so high. In this straightforward primer, complete with discussion questions, Professor Kimball invites us all to class. Attendance is required if we are to survive. Take. Read. Understand. Repeat. It is hard to imagine a more timely book."

—**Rev. Robin Meyers,** PhD, Senior Minister of Mayflower Congregational UCC Church, Oklahoma City; Distinguished Professor Emeritus of Philosophy, Oklahoma City University; and author of *Saving God from Religion: A Minister's Search for Faith in a Skeptical Age*

"Charles Kimball has done it yet again: in this concise exploration of Christian-Muslim relations, he provides a map through the contemporary morass of stereotypes and misinformation about Islam, a lack of understanding and respect, and a myopic and distorted view of Islam as a religion that is inherently evil and violent. *Truth over Fear* will indispensably serve a wide audience of persons who want to learn more about Muslims and their faith and actions, and it will nurture more constructive relations between the world's two largest religions. Toward that end, Dr. Kimball challenges misunderstandings of Islam and seeks to root out deep biases about Muslims that stoke fear and anger."

—**Rev. Clifford Chalmers Cain,** PhD, Harrod-C.S. Lewis Professor of Religious Studies, Westminster College

"I can think of no more eloquent or accessible guide to combating popular untruths about Islam than Charles Kimball. A lifelong student of world religions, theologically nimble, deeply knowledgeable of the Qur'an, and experienced in dialogue and the politics of the Middle East, this Baptist scholar offers a pathway for Christians to engage Islam with insight and respect. A long concern of the author has been how religion is used to justify destructive behavior, and in this latest offering, Kimball provides a voice that our fraught times urgently need to hear."

—**Molly T. Marshall,** PhD, President and Professor of Theology and Spiritual Formation, Central Baptist Theological Seminary

"There are very few Christian scholars of Islam whose education, experience, and engagement with Muslims qualify them as the most trustworthy resources for understanding and relating to the second-largest religion in the world. Among Catholics, John Esposito is that person, while among Protestants, Charles Kimball is the one to whom Christians should turn. With clear, compelling prose Kimball provides doctrinal explanation, historical overview, biblical and theological insight, and interfaith perspective to counter the fear and misinformation perpetuated by Islamophobia. Helpful, thought-provoking discussion questions at the end of each chapter make this highly recommended book extremely useful for both individual and group learning."

—**Robert P. Sellers,** former Chair, Parliament of the World's
Religions; Professor Emeritus of Theology and Connally Chair
of Missions Emeritus, Hardin-Simmons University

"With his *Truth over Fear,* Charles Kimball continues the journey begun in his earlier works, *When Religion Becomes Evil* and *When Religion Becomes Lethal,* mapping the tripwires that often erupt in religion-inspired conflict. This time, though, he specifically and helpfully focuses on Christian-Muslim relations and—as a scholar committed to the life of local communities of faith—helps Christians identify and depose the lies that stand in the way of genuine interfaith respect (and, maybe, affection) in ways that can heal the larger tears in our social fabric."

—**Ken Sehested,** curator of prayerandpolitiks.org and coauthor
of *Peace Primer II: Quotes from Jewish, Christian,*
and Islamic Scripture and Tradition

"With wisdom born through vast experience and deep hope, Dr. Kimball invites us to engage heart and mind as we learn and discern what is true and best in our faith traditions. In a time when fear passes for fact, *Truth over Fear* provides a depth of information and a way for conversation and actions to build bridges of understanding and pathways for peace."

—**Rev. David Spain,** Senior Minister,
First Christian Church, Norman, Oklahoma

"This excellent book is a valuable guide for interfaith education and conversation. Drawing on his scholarly expertise in both Islamic and Christian studies, Professor Charles Kimball provides insightful information from both faiths, while challenging certain misrepresentations that often contribute to mistrust and animosity. To call its publication *timely* is an understatement."

—**Bill J. Leonard,** Dunn Professor Emeritus of Baptist
Studies and Church History, Wake Forest University

"Dr. Charles Kimball creates a powerful new paradigm for people of goodwill seeking the truth about Islam. Focusing on building community, Dr. Kimball provides a path for goodwill Christians and Muslims to learn from one another and embark on a collaborative effort for a more hopeful tomorrow."

—**Rev. Dr. R. Mitch Randall,** Executive Director, EthicsDaily.com

"Dr. Charles Kimball's newest volume, *Truth over Fear: Combating the Lies about Islam,* is his most extensive and significant book since the publication of his post-9/11 volumes *When Religion Becomes Evil* and *When Religion Becomes Lethal.* There is no one in America more knowledgeable about the hopes and fears of Islam in the twenty-first century and how other nations and faith traditions can relate to this second-largest religion in the world. All of his six chapters reveal a deep and insightful message about how Islam has grown, why it is misunderstood by so many people, and what Muslims, Jews, Christians, and others can do to build bridges instead of barriers. The last chapter, titled 'Peaceful Coexistence and Cooperation in a Dangerous World: Living into a Healthy and Hopeful Future,' provides a visionary outlook, a theological framework, and a practical approach to healing old wounds and learning to live together in peace. And the questions for discussion at the end of each chapter are accessible to large audiences, small groups, and individuals who desire to move forward instead of remaining resistant to the keys that can help to unlock discernment and dialogue for the future. This book can and will have a profound impact on all those who read it and choose to share it with a wider constituency."

—Dr. George B. Wirth, Pastor Emeritus,
First Presbyterian Church, Atlanta, Georgia

"Charles Kimball has a lifetime of interfaith ministry, scholarly investigation, insightful teaching, and patient modeling for the task of building bridges of peace and understanding between Muslims and Christians. He now brings a goldmine of valuable historical and religious information to correct misinformation and help persons of both religions grow in their understanding and respect of each other. He brings a healing word and a tool for further healing in a time when it is desperately needed."

—Richard Olsen, Professor Emeritus of Pastoral Theology,
Central Baptist Theological Seminary; author of *Side by Side:*
Being Christian in a Multifaith World

"We live in an interconnected and highly interdependent world, one that is increasingly susceptible to fear, false narratives, mounting mistrust, and religious bias. It is inside this context that Dr. Charles Kimball calls for a new way of thinking and engaging one another. *Truth over Fear* provides a light of understanding on the complexities of today, pointing to a new moment of vision, a world that all faith traditions value."

—Rev. Dr. Jonathan Barton, former General Minister
of the Virginia Council of Churches

"A wise and timely guide for Muslim-Christian relations, richly informed by years of study, experience, and engagement with Muslims both internationally and locally. Evocative questions at the end of each chapter make the book a perfect tool for interfaith dialogue in mosques and churches."

—E. Glenn Hinson, Professor Emeritus of Church History,
Baptist Theological Seminary at Richmond

"Drawing on rich personal, professional, and scholarly experience, Charles Kimball offers a vital and compelling on-ramp to demystifying Islam and supporting positive Christian-Muslim relations. Grounded in Christian biblical mandates, he gets to the heart of Islam and many of the roots of our fears of

Islam, while not avoiding tough conversations about doctrinal differences and histories of violence. Exceedingly accessible, this book is a welcome resource for Christian clergy and laity seeking to educate themselves about Islam and interfaith dialogue. The timing could not be more important; these are the peacemaking conversations to which we are called, and Kimball walks gently but assuredly alongside those beginning the journey."

—**C. Melissa Snarr,** Associate Professor of Ethics
and Society, Vanderbilt Divinity School

"In *Truth over Fear: Combating the Lies about Islam,* Charles Kimball has once again given us a great gift. Professor Kimball offers us the challenge to better understand Islam and to be wary of rampant and uninformed Islamophobia. He points out the dangerous consequences of misinformation, fear, and prejudice not least among them. His call for a new paradigm offers us great hope. Having known Charles since his first days as a graduate student at Harvard, and having worked with him closely during the U.S.-Iran hostage crisis, I am well aware of his lifelong commitment to a more peaceful world through engagement and deeper understanding. This book is the result of that lifelong journey. I cannot imagine a better guide than Charles Kimball."

—**John Walsh,** Omer E. Robbins Chaplain to the University of Redlands
and Director of the Jameson Center for the Study of Religion and Ethics

"In this book Charles Kimball addresses a critically important topic with expertise and sensitivity. As one who works in contexts of severe Christian and Muslim extremism and conflict, I am deeply aware of how narrow theologies of exclusivity and attitudes of superiority hinder efforts at peacemaking. This highly readable and useful volume will no doubt make a significant contribution toward broadening Christian theological notions and alleviating misconceptions and fears about Islam."

—**Rev. Dr. Shanta Premawardhana,** President,
OMNIA Institute for Contextual Leadership

"At a time when a chorus of strident voices seems to point to Islam on a daily basis as the root of all evil, Charles Kimball's new book offers clarity and insight. Kimball provides an informative overview of Islam; an immensely helpful history of Muslim-Christian relations, including a thorough analysis of the geopolitical shifts of the last half century in the Middle East and their implications for interfaith and multinational relationships; and an assessment of current challenges and future opportunities. He faces head-on the distortions within Islam, Christianity, and other faiths that lead to conflict and violence. He charts a path with practical help for the faithful to engage in interfaith dialogue without giving up their missionary calling, a way to respect other views without succumbing to theological relativism—with the minimal goal of not bearing false witness against our neighbor and the lofty goal of increasing the love of God and neighbor (teachings common to all three Abrahamic faiths). My hope is that

Truth over Fear will reach a broad audience of clergy and laity, elected officials and ordinary citizens, Christians and Muslims, and others. Our shared future may depend on a willingness to engage the subject matter of this book."
—**Dr. Christopher C. F. Chapman,** Pastor,
First Baptist Church, Raleigh, North Carolina

"Charles Kimball's latest book, *Truth over Fear*, is a timely and concise read on Islam and the Muslim-Christian relationship, which should not only be in every pastor's library but also read widely by non-clergy in order to combat the general lack of understanding among Americans about the world's second-largest religion."
—**Rev. Dr. Robert S. Rice,** former Senior Minister,
First Presbyterian Church, Norman, Oklahoma

"'But what can I do?' well-meaning Christians often ask when confronted with the Islamophobia that permeates our nation. For starters, we could read Charles Kimball's informative book *Truth over Fear*. Not only will we receive an overview of Islam and the story of Muslim-Christian interchange through the last six hundred years, we will also gain the resources we need for not bearing false witness against our neighbors, for loving our neighbors, and for living peaceably with all our neighbors into a future marked by respect and care rather than hate and harm."
—**Nancy Claire Pittman,** President and Stephen J. England Associate
Professor of the Practice of Ministry, Phillips Theological Seminary

"In today's academy, religious studies professors seldom address theological questions so directly and with such insight as Charles Kimball. His book is urgently needed, not only to correct our dangerous misconceptions about Islam but also to challenge simplistic understandings of religion held by persons of faith and agnostics alike. Kimball guides even those with little background through complex issues and in the process opens up whole new ways to think about a meaningful life of faith."
—**Helen Lee Turner,** Reuben B. Pitts Professor
of Religion, Furman University

Truth over Fear

Truth over Fear

Combating the Lies about Islam

CHARLES KIMBALL

WESTMINSTER
JOHN KNOX PRESS
LOUISVILLE · KENTUCKY

First edition
Published by Westminster John Knox Press
Louisville, Kentucky

19 20 21 22 23 24 25 26 27 28—10 9 8 7 6 5 4 3 2 1

Unless otherwise identified, Scripture quotations are from the New Revised Standard Version of the Bible, are copyright © 1989 by the Division of Christian Education of the National Council of the Churches of Christ in the U.S.A., and are used by permission.

Most quotations from the Qur'an are the author's translations and are identified as such by "auth. trans." Quotations from the Qur'an that are not the author's translations are from *The Study Quran: A New Translation and Commentary,* Seyyed Hossein Nasr, Caner K. Dagli, Maria Massi Dakake, Joseph E. B Lumbard, and Mohammed Rustom, eds. (Harper-Collins: New York, 2015).

Book design by Sharon Adams
Cover design by Nita Ybarra and Allison Taylor

Library of Congress Cataloging-in-Publication Data
Names: Kimball, Charles, author.
Title: Truth over fear : combating the lies about Islam / Charles A. Kimball.
Description: First edition. | Louisville, Kentucky : Westminster John Knox Press, 2019.
  | Includes bibliographical references and index.
Identifiers: LCCN 2019005261 (print) | ISBN 9780664264628 (pbk. : alk. paper)
Subjects: LCSH: Islam—Relations—Christianity. | Christianity and other Religions—
  Islam. | Islam—Doctrines.
Classification: LCC BP172 .K633 2019 (print) | LCC BP172 (ebook) |
  DDC 261.2/7—dc23
LC record available at https://lccn.loc.gov/2019005261
LC ebook record available at https://lccn.loc.gov/2019980859

♾ The paper used in this publication meets the minimum requirements
of the American National Standard for Information Sciences—Permanence
of Paper for Printed Library Materials, ANSI Z39.48–1992.

For Jane Idleman Smith, Diana Eck, and John Carman—
mentors and friends on a lifelong journey toward
interfaith understanding, dialogue, and cooperation

Contents

Acknowledgments

This book draws on research, insights, and experiences over four decades. There are many people who deserve recognition for their numerous contributions along the way. Many scholars have enriched my understanding through academic study of Islam (and other religious traditions); many others have helped develop and refine my perspectives through engagement in interfaith dialogue in local, national, and international settings; a few have been mentors and colleagues with whom I've shared the journey in both contexts—the academic world of higher education and interfaith dialogue programs. The three mentors and friends to whom this book is dedicated are in this latter group. I'll say more about these three in the final paragraphs below.

I have had the great good fortune of working at eight institutions whose leaders encouraged, affirmed, and supported my vocation. Throughout the 1980s, I was based in New York but working nationally and internationally as Interfaith Director at the Fellowship of Reconciliation and Middle East Director at the National Council of Churches. I'm forever grateful for professors, deans, provosts, presidents, and other administrators at Oklahoma State, the Southern Baptist Theological Seminary, Harvard, Furman, and Wake Forest Universities. Since 2008, I've enjoyed the congenial and supportive environment at the University of Oklahoma, including a sabbatical leave that enabled me to complete this book.

My clear indebtedness to some individuals in these and other settings is reflected in the text and notes. Many others will not be readily apparent, most notably people in hundreds of colleges, universities, seminaries, divinity schools, churches, mosques, and synagogues where I've been invited to speak over the years. Several people have offered valuable suggestions and correctives in the process of developing and refining portions of this book. I am deeply grateful to Wesley Ariarajah, John Borelli, Chris Chapman, Imad Enchassi, John Esposito, Jalal Farzaneh, Mohammad Farzaneh, Mary Foskett, Khalid Griggs, Scott Hudgins, Robin Meyers, Tom Michel, Bob Rice, Jeff Rogers, Muzammil Siddiqi, David Spain, Helen Lee Turner, John Walsh, and George Wirth. I am particularly appreciative of the wise guidance, constructive collaboration, and longstanding friendship I enjoy with Steve Hanselman of LevelFive Media.

No author could hope for more helpful professionals than those with whom I've worked at Westminster John Knox Press, most notably Dan Braden and Elle D. Rogers. I am particularly grateful to Bob Ratcliff, who has guided my work on this book from start to finish. Bob helped both to frame larger issues and fine-tune points with invaluable editorial suggestions at every step along the way.

Writing a book is for me both solitary enterprise and a family project. For nearly half a century, my spouse, Nancy, has been my best friend, confidant, sounding board, and loving critic. Her support and forbearance continue to sustain me on a life journey that neither of us could have predicted when we were married in Stillwater, Oklahoma, as seniors in college.

Finally allow me a brief word about how my relationship developed with the three mentors and friends to whom this book is dedicated: Jane Idleman Smith, Diana Eck, and John Carman. When Nancy and I arrived in Cambridge, Massachusetts, to begin my doctoral program in the summer of 1975, we moved into Harvard's Center for the Study of World Religions (CSWR). At that time, the CSWR was both an academic center and an experiential learning experiment in which doctoral students studying world religions and scholars—both from Harvard and visiting scholars from around the world—lived side by side in the center's twenty apartments. In addition to engaging one another in classes and doctoral seminars, we shared meals, celebrated holidays, and interacted in our daily routines with students from different religious traditions as well as brilliant scholars, including Wilfred Cantwell Smith, George Rupp, and Bill Graham. We enjoyed visits and opportunities to engage world-renowned figures such as the Dalai Lama, Huston Smith, Seyyed Hossein Nasr, W. Montgomery Watt, and Dastur Khotwal—the High Priest of Zoroastrianism. Those of us who lived and worked at the CSWR for many years were fortunate in too many ways to count.

In 1975, John Carman and Jane Smith were faculty members at Harvard Divinity School while also serving as director and associate director, respectively, at the CSWR. Diana Eck was in her final year of dissertation work, after which she was immediately appointed to the Harvard faculty where she has had an illustrious career as a teacher-scholar with a national and global outreach. Like all faculty members at Harvard, Jane, John, and Diana all exemplified and demanded the highest standards for scholarly work. At the same time, all three were deeply committed to going out from the university in pursuit of constructive interfaith dialogue initiatives in the "real" world. From the moment I arrived and to this day, John, Diana, and Jane have been mentors, cherished friends, and exemplary models in interfaith understanding, dialogue, and cooperation. With love and a grateful heart, I dedicate this book to Diana, Jane, and John.

Introduction

Politicians, preachers, and many in the media constantly portray Islam as somehow inherently violent and menacing. The deliberate dissemination of misinformation and outright lies about Islam is rampant, and it is getting worse, not better. The alarming message repeatedly conveyed is unambiguous: "Be afraid. Be very afraid."

Frightening images are daily engrained in far-reaching ways. Who among the readers of this book has not received emails forwarded by an uncle or a friend that purport to unmask the "true" goal of all Muslims as world domination, the plot to impose Sharia (Islamic law), and/or the Qur'anic mandate that Muslims kill all the Jews and Christians? The people fanning the flames of Islamophobia—whether in the national spotlight or operating in innumerable local settings—are willfully uninformed or disingenuous or both. Whether the politicians, preachers, and self-appointed pundits are sincere or cynical, their blatant efforts effectively exacerbate fears as they disseminate misinformation and confusion about the world's second-largest religion. Wittingly or unwittingly, they add an explosive component in the twenty-first-century world, where many turbulent forces and events are already in the mix.

Stoking fear and anger has real-world consequences. Increasingly, the hostility directed toward Muslims threatens their physical safety. Public harassment of individuals and families as well as threats and malicious attacks on mosques continue to rise in the United States and other Christian-majority countries. The brutal slaughter of more than fifty Muslims during Friday prayers at two mosques in Christchurch, New Zealand, in March of 2019 was a sickening reminder that anti-Muslim sentiment can embolden extremists to perpetrate vicious hate crimes.

There is another lie about Islam at the other end of the spectrum. Many Muslims and some non-Muslims repeat the mantra "Islam is a religion of peace" and seem to think that this assertion ends the discussion. They dismiss anyone or any group claiming inspiration from Islam who justify violence or extremism as not being "true Muslims." Religion is more complex than that. One has to take seriously and wrestle with what is going on when a significant minority of believers within a religion justifies violence in ways that defy what is claimed to be the very heart of the religion. Muslims cannot simply write off frustrated, angry, and even violent extremists who present themselves as devout Muslims any more than Christians can dismiss Crusaders or the Ku Klux Klan or the untold millions of Christians who have acted harshly toward Jews, Muslims, and other Christians for two thousand years. Most Christians readily affirm that Jesus taught a gospel of love. But the actual behavior of many Christians through the centuries frequently has failed to manifest that ideal.

In our increasingly interconnected and interdependent world community, heightened fear, misinformation, widespread distrust, and religious prejudice make the dangers we face more ominous than ever. By far, the most widespread and explosive dynamics converge today around Christian-Muslim relations. Christianity is the world's largest religion, with more than two billion adherents. Islam is second with more than 1.7 billion followers. Christians and Muslims together comprise roughly one-half of the world's population.[1] They are the most widespread religions geographically and the fastest growing. This much is clear: the ways in which Christians and Muslims relate to one another in coming years will have profound consequences on both communities—and for the world.

Put another way, the twenty-first century may well be defined by interfaith relationships. The new century began with a horrifying event that also served as a dire harbinger if the status quo persists. The terrorist attacks on September 11, 2001, underscored the far-reaching ramifications of ideological conflict nourished by religious extremists who are prepared to die as they lash out. People everywhere recognized immediately how small numbers of religious zealots are able to wreak havoc on a global scale, even without access to the most frightening weapons on earth. Fortunately, the hijackers on that fateful morning did not have nuclear, chemical, or biological weapons. Instead they crafted a sinister plan: using box knives they turned commercial airliners into weapons of mass destruction. However horribly misguided they were, they were true believers in their cause. The papers left behind by their leader, Muhammad Atta, indicated that he and others were expecting a heavenly reward for their actions. Religion is a powerful and pervasive force that has too often been used to justify destructive behavior. In the twenty-first century, however, the stakes are much higher for more people than ever before. Destructive actions are no longer isolated geographically or largely unknown due to limited means of disseminating news.

Religions are also complex. The major religious traditions that have stood the test of time cannot be reduced to a caricature by outsiders or by insiders. To do so is by definition simplistic and therefore highly misleading. The enduring religions that have inspired and nurtured the lives of hundreds of millions of people for many centuries are always changing and adapting in both subtle and substantial ways. Any thoughtful study of Judaism, Christianity, Islam, or the Hindu and Buddhist traditions reveals varying interpretations that lead to the creation of new subgroups or sects as well as movements for reform. For far too many non-Muslims in the West, however, the diversity and complexity evident in all world religions doesn't seem to apply Muslims. Instead, simplistic stereotypes of Islam, Muslims, and "core" teachings in the Qur'an abound. The result is a caricature of Islam and Muslims that often reflects the highly visible actions of extremists and revolutionaries.

Developing a New Paradigm

What Western Christians and others of goodwill desperately need is a new paradigm, a new way of thinking about Islam and engaging Muslims. This paradigm includes a fair-minded approach to Islam that is grounded on compelling biblical mandates. For people of goodwill who wouldn't normally look to the Bible for guidance, these mandates can still be seen as wise and pragmatic. This book seeks to provide that paradigm by dispelling widespread fears and inaccurate perceptions about Islam and Muslims. Clarifying truths can markedly diminish the incendiary and accusatory attitudes and rhetoric inexorably leading to more conflict. Accurate information and a healthier perspective go a long way toward calming fears about the "other." But combating lies with trustworthy information is not enough. People who wish to be good citizens, good neighbors, and/or agents of reconciliation also need to know what, specifically, they can do to contribute constructively toward a more hopeful and healthy future in local, national, and international settings. Happily, there is a lot we can do as individuals and as communities of faith to work toward that more hopeful future.

There are several primary audiences for whom this book is presented, including the following: Christian clergy, adult study groups in churches, and individual Christians who want to break through the fear and confusion about Islam. In my experience, when Christians develop a more accurate understanding of Islam, they want to nurture more constructive relationships with Muslims in their communities. This book is also intended for the substantial number of people not affiliated with a local congregation who seek to be good neighbors and good citizens. Many Muslims and other people of goodwill will also find the book to be useful in various ways even as they provide feedback and a critique of what is being presented.

I offer this book not as a detached academic observer but as one who has been deeply engaged with the subject matter throughout my adult life. I am a Christian, an ecumenically committed Baptist member of the clergy for more than four decades. I am also a student of world religions, a university and divinity school professor of comparative religion with specialization in Islamic studies and Christian-Muslim relations. I have taught students from many faith communities along with many who describe themselves as atheists, agnostics, and a growing number affirming they are "spiritual but not religious." A good portion of my professional life has involved actively working with Christians, Muslims, and Jews at the intersections of religion, politics, and interfaith dialogue in the U.S., Europe, and Middle East. Since the mid-1970s, this work has included teaching, lecturing, writing articles and books, presenting sermons, and engaging in public dialogue programs in more than five hundred universities, seminaries, churches, mosques, and synagogues in North America and abroad. I have also given more than one thousand interviews for local, national, and international television, radio, and print journalists over the years.

In 1977–78 my spouse and I lived in Cairo, Egypt, as part of my doctoral program at Harvard University. We were in Egypt and traveling around the Middle East during the time when Egypt's president, Anwar Sadat, traveled to Jerusalem to begin what became the Camp David peace process. In the following year, at age twenty-nine, I was one of seven—six Christian clergy and one former Peace Corps volunteer—invited to Iran to meet with the Ayatollah Khomeini, many religious and political leaders, and the student militants occupying the U.S. embassy and holding fifty-three Americans hostage in the early weeks of the Iran hostage crisis. Apart from an Iranian American academic and journalist, we were the only seven Americans who met with Ayatollah Khomeini during what turned out to be a 444-day crisis. I returned to Iran at the invitation of Iranian leaders and with the quiet support of the U.S. State Department on two other occasions, for a total of two months. The Rev. John Walsh, a chaplain at Princeton University at the time, and I were able to take mail to the American hostages and meet with Iranian religious and political leaders as well as the students occupying the U.S. embassy throughout the lengthy ordeal.

Throughout the 1980s, I served as Middle East Director for the National Council of Churches, based in New York. In that role, I coordinated the mission and service ministries of many Protestant and Orthodox American denominations working in the Middle East. That decade included a great deal of turmoil and conflict on several fronts: the Iran-Iraq war, the Israeli invasion of Lebanon and subsequent occupation of Southern Lebanon, the multisided and convoluted conflict in that tiny land, and the ongoing Israeli-Palestinian conflict. The following chapters include selected illustrations from my work over the years when these elucidate key issues or points being presented.

Some years ago, an insightful friend offered wise words that are particularly applicable to the precarious time in which we are living: "When you are standing on the edge of a cliff, progress is not defined as one step forward!" The way forward first requires a step backward, away from the precipice. The structure of this book is informed by this image. It is wise to consider the major factors that have brought us to the brink. To be sure, the traumatic events on 9/11 and subsequent upheavals and emergence of extremist groups provide the immediate context. But the turbulent developments of the past two decades didn't happen in a vacuum. They occurred and continue to develop in the context of both a deep history and more recent upheavals lodged in the second half of the twentieth century.

A clearer understanding of the world in which we are living today is needed if we hope to fashion a positive way forward in our all too quarrelsome human family. The chapters that follow focus on these essential components: reflection on Islamic self-understanding and highlighting priorities shared with Christians and others; an overview of key features shaping Christian-Muslim relations over the centuries; and an analysis of formative developments that are shaping the often-volatile contemporary dynamics. Fortunately, the way forward is not blocked for people of faith and goodwill. The final two chapters of the book center

on ways Christians and others can and should move forward constructively in the midst of religious pluralism.

Chapter 1 explicates why and how Islamophobia is increasing and the biblical principles on which people of faith can and
should base their attitudes and actions if we hope to live into a
less dangerous world in the coming decades.

Chapter One

The Peril and Promise of Interfaith Relations in the Twenty-First Century

> The world is too dangerous for anything but truth and too small for anything but love.
> The Rev. William Sloane Coffin Jr.

Confusion and Fear of Islam Rises at the End of the Twentieth Century

Christians and Muslims have traveled a long, often circuitous and bumpy road together for more than fourteen centuries. In the latter half of the twentieth century, several unsettling and confusing developments served to heighten fear and confusion about Muslims and Islam among non-Muslims in the West. A brief overview helps us comprehend why the anti-Islamic pronouncements by political, religious, and media figures have found such a receptive audience.

The 1979 Iranian revolution and subsequent 444-day hostage crisis was a major turning point. This unexpected revolution sent jarring shock waves throughout the Middle East and around the world. On December 31, 1977, President Jimmy Carter boldly declared Iran to be "an island of stability in one of the more troubled areas of the world." He then praised the Shah of Iran "for your leadership and the great respect, admiration, and love which your people give to you."[1] Less than a year later, over 90 percent of the Iranian people rose up to oust the Shah. Iran, geographically situated in the soft underbelly of the former Soviet Union, was so intimately connected to the U.S. that former Secretary of State Henry Kissinger famously called the Shah "the rarest of leaders, an unconditional ally."[2] If a leader fully backed by a superpower, a man with phenomenal wealth, a state-of-the art military, and a brutal secret police could be toppled by a popular, nonviolent revolution where millions took to the streets and their rooftops to declare "*Allahu akbar!*" (God is most great!), how secure could any other dictatorial or hereditary leader be? Their fear that the Iranian revolution might spread led leaders in Jordan, Egypt, Saudi Arabia, the United States, and other countries to support Iraq and its brutal dictator, Saddam Hussein, throughout the decade-long Iran-Iraq War in the 1980s. While many groups combined in opposition to the Shah, the Ayatollah Khomeini became the public face of the revolution, and his faction won out in the subsequent struggle for power in the newly formed Islamic Republic of Iran. The massive influence of Ayatollah Khomeini led *Time* magazine to name him "Man of the Year" for 1979. The image of Khomeini on the cover of *Time* on January 7, 1980, looks somewhat demonic. He was becoming the face of a religion to be feared.

Ironically, the United States' position on Muslim revolutionaries in Iran's neighboring country, Afghanistan, was quite different. There the principle that "the enemy of my enemy is my friend" guided the policy and rhetoric. The *mujahidin* (revolutionary Islamic fighters) in Afghanistan were opposing the then-Soviet-backed regime while Soviet troops occupied the country. In a broadcast seen around the world, President Carter's National Security Advisor, Zbigniew Brzezinski, was shown holding up a rifle as he stood in rugged terrain among the Afghan "freedom fighters," declaring that theirs was a just cause and God was on their side. Usama bin Ladin was one of the leaders who had traveled to Afghanistan to join in this fight against Soviet forces. Years later, of course, the same people whom the U.S. supported in their revolutionary struggle against the Soviets became the leaders of the Taliban and al-Qaida.

The Iran hostage crisis launched a new era of intensive media coverage. In the pre-cable television era, the traditional thirty-minute evening news programs on ABC, CBS, NBC, and PBS strained to cover the intense drama of the hostage crisis. ABC News then launched a new nightly program on November 8, 1979, just four days after the U.S. embassy in Tehran was taken over by student militants. Initially called "The Iran Crisis: America Held Hostage," the Monday through Friday nightly program drew large audiences. The program was subsequently renamed *Nightline*. After the hostages were released, *Nightline* remained in the 11:30 p.m. EST time slot. Since I was involved directly in the Iranian hostage drama, I followed events very closely. I vividly recall when executives at ABC announced that they would continue the *Nightline* program when the hostage crisis was over. When asked about the decision, two key points were cited. *Nightline* was the first ABC program to compete effectively for viewers at the 11:30 p.m. EST time slot where Johnny Carson's *Tonight Show* dominated. A second rationale was the conviction that there would be a crisis somewhere in the world that will require in-depth reporting. A new era was dawning as short local and national news programs were being supplemented by extended coverage of whatever was most dramatic and sensational on a given day. Today, the explosion of media outlets with multiple 24/7 news channels and social media enabled by the Internet has changed the situation in ways that were unimaginable forty years ago. One mantra still dictates priorities: "If it bleeds, it leads."

The 1980s and 1990s saw a small, but growing number of revolutionary groups and militant extremists emerge in several countries; some periodically attacked U.S. embassies in Lebanon, Pakistan, and Saudi Arabia and also the USS *Cole* off the coast of Yemen. During this time groups like Hizbullah (Party of God) in Lebanon and HAMAS (Islamic Resistance Movement) in Gaza received a great deal of attention in the Western press as the militant military branches of the unofficial governments within governments combined defiant proclamations with stepped-up attacks on Israeli forces occupying their lands. The terrifying pictures in the aftermath of car bombs, suicide attackers, or explosives placed on buses or in crowded marketplaces—especially in Lebanon, Israel/Palestine, and years later in Iraq—understandably stoked already-existing fears and perceptions about forces at work within Muslim-majority countries.

In February of 1993, the context shifted to New York City when an extremist group headed by the blind Egyptian cleric Umar Abdul Rahman attempted to bomb the World Trade Center. While this assault was largely unsuccessful, the fact that it occurred in the U.S. set off a new alarm. Eight years later came the stunning terrorist attacks on the World Trade Center and Pentagon.

The high visibility of al-Qaida and the emergence of other extremist groups like ISIS (The Islamic State in Syria/Iraq; sometimes called ISIL, The Islamic State in the Levant), al-Shabab (meaning "The Youth," a group aligned with al-Qaida) in Somalia, and Boko Haram (meaning "Westernization is forbidden," a branch of ISIS) in Nigeria further served to connect extremism with Islam in the minds of many. People identified as representatives of these and other groups perpetrated deplorable acts both to call attention to their cause and to create fear and hysteria locally and beyond. While a few connections exist between these groups, each has been shaped by its own local context and history. Other despicable and gruesome images reported after attacks in European cities further reinforce the generic linking of Islam with violence: small groups of extremists placing bombs on London subways and buses; the mass murder of concertgoers in Paris and hapless passengers at the international airport in Brussels; and the horrifying attacks by so-called lone wolves who deliberately drive trucks or cars into crowds of unsuspecting civilians.

While these and other militant groups represent a small fraction on the fringes of self-identifying Muslims, their various deplorable actions consistently receive the massive media attention that terrorists and extremists always seek. Such groups cannot be ignored or dismissed. They are part of the larger picture and represent real and present dangers both to those who are nearby and to the wider world community. No one knows with certainty how many violent extremists exist among the world's 1.7+ billion Muslims. Even if that number were 500,000 or one million, that is far less than 1 percent. And yet, as the nineteen people who hijacked four planes on 9/11 made clear, it doesn't take many people to do great harm.

The Muslim Brotherhood is a large organization with several branches, each possessing its own history and character. It emerged during the past century as a reformist group in Egypt, the Sudan, Jordan, and Syria. For many Americans, the Muslim Brotherhood has become shorthand for those who long to see Islam as the basis for government in their countries. While the Muslim Brotherhood neither explains nor accounts for many of the actions connected with the groups noted above, it has had profound influence, particularly through the writings of Sayyid Qutb (Quṭb),[3] one of the Brotherhood's key figures. Qutb's experiences in the U.S. produced a strong revulsion for Western decadence. This was combined with a deep disdain for the corrupt leaders in Egypt and other Muslim-majority countries and led him to develop a blueprint for reform, including the use of violence if necessary. The large majority of Muslim Brothers advocate gradual political change by working through existing systems. But some—from the leaders of al-Jihad, the group that assassinated Anwar Sadat, to Usama bin Ladin and his successor, the Egyptian physician Ayman al-Zawahiri—initially found their justification for violence in the work of Sayyid Qutb.

It is understandable how many otherwise well-intentioned non-Muslims have embraced simplistic, stereotypical images of Islam and Muslims. Inundated with images from the Iran hostage crisis and Hizbullah's war against Israel to the al-Qaida-led attacks on 9/11 and the gruesome decapitation of Western hostages by ISIS murderers on YouTube, many are susceptible to a view that lumps all of this together as though these are somehow one and the same thing. By 2010, growing generic fear of Islam in the U.S. prompted *Time* magazine to run a cover story posing this question: "Is America Islamophobic?" In broad terms, the answer to that question is clear: "Yes!"

Politicians and Preachers Reinforce Islamophobia

One of the most memorable ways Donald Trump grabbed the media spotlight in his campaign for the presidency occurred on December 7, 2015. Trump released a statement and then read it publicly. He called for a "total and complete shutdown of Muslims entering the United States until our country's representatives can figure out what the hell is going on." He went on to say, "We have no choice," and emphasized that "we must look at mosques" because "there is anger within them." The reaction to this pronouncement was swift and strong from many quarters, but it didn't dissuade Trump as he apparently believed his prescriptions were politically advantageous. The *New York Times* reported that his earlier calls for a database to track Muslims in America and his repeated citations of the discredited rumors that "thousands of Muslims in New Jersey celebrated on 9/11" had boosted his poll numbers.[4]

Within a week after taking the oath of office, President Trump issued an Executive Order titled "Protecting the Nation from Foreign Terrorist Entry into the United States." This action prompted tens of thousands of protesters to take to the streets, gather at airports across the country, and demonstrate in front of the offices of Homeland Security.[5] The action was widely perceived, sharply criticized, and initially struck down in court as an intentional ban on Muslims. This set off a yearlong court battle including refinements and appeals designed to stay within the letter of the law on when the exercise of presidential authority and the constitutional mandates were at odds.

On November 27, 2017, Trump casually and impulsively disseminated an anti-Islamic communication that engendered immediate and sharply critical reactions on an international scale. On that day, he re-tweeted three anti-Muslim videos produced by Britain First, a well-known far-right hate group in England. At the time, Trump had some 44 million daily followers on Twitter. The first video claimed to show a Muslim migrant beating up a Dutch boy on crutches. The second was labeled "Muslim destroys a statue of the Virgin Mary." The third read, "Islamist mob pushes teenage boy off roof and beats him to death." At the time of the tweet, all three videos had been proved to be either misleading or untruthful. Within twenty-four hours, British Prime Minister Theresa May issued a strong rebuke of Trump for having re-tweeted vile and false materials from a well-known hate group. The Archbishop of Canterbury also communicated his dismay at Trump's "deeply disturbing" decision to amplify the voices of far-right extremists and called on the president to make clear his opposition to racism and hatred in all forms. London's mayor, Sadiq Khan, also denounced Britain First as "a vile, hate-fueled organization whose views should be condemned, not amplified." Khan joined with several members of the government in calling on the prime minister to rescind the invitation for Trump to come to the UK in 2018.[6]

Other high-profile political figures like Mike Huckabee, the former Arkansas governor and two-time presidential candidate, and Newt Gingrich, the former Speaker of the U.S. House of Representatives, have made uninformed and derogatory public pronouncements about Islam. On his national radio program in 2013, for instance, Huckabee prefaced inflammatory remarks by declaring, "[It is] politically incorrect to say anything unkind about Islam." Huckabee then said this:

> Can someone explain to me why it is that we tiptoe around a religion that promotes the most murderous mayhem on the planet in their so-called "holiest days"? . . . Muslims will go to the mosque, and they will have their day of prayer, and they come out of there like uncorked animals—throwing rocks and burning cars.[7]

In the aftermath of a terrorist attack that killed eighty-four people in Nice, France, Newt Gingrich proposed a "test" for every Muslim and then advocated deportation for all who believe in Sharia. Gingrich apparently had no idea what Sharia is or how observant Muslims naturally seek to follow Islamic law in their personal lives. No matter, his clarion call had the desired effect by painting Muslims with a broad brush.[8]

Employing Sharia as a buzzword is often in plain sight. On March 9, 2019, for example, prominent FOX News host Jeanine Pirro suggested adherence to Sharia is antithetical to the U.S. Constitution. Her tirade focused on the U.S. Representative from Minnesota, Ilhan Omar, one of the first two Muslim women elected to Congress. Pirro began her popular television program, *Justice with Judge Jeanine*, with these words:

> Omar wears a hijab, which, according to the Koran 33:59, tells women to cover so they won't get molested. Is her adherence to this Islamic doctrine indicative of her adherence to Sharia law, which in itself is antithetical to the United States Constitution?[9]

Think for a moment. Orthodox Jewish women wear a head covering. When I was growing up, Catholic nuns universally wore head coverings as part of their habit. Would anyone suggest that nuns or Orthodox Jewish women following their religious convictions with attire that included head covering were somehow automatically against the U.S. Constitution?

There are many more pronouncements by these and numerous other political leaders. In the 2018 special election for an open U.S. Senate seat in Alabama, for instance, Roy Moore, the Republican candidate and former Chief Justice of the Alabama Supreme Court, declared that Muslims should not be allowed to be seated in the U.S. Congress because they have to take the oath of office on a Christian Bible. In fact, no one has to take the oath on a Christian Bible. Four years earlier, Moore opined: "The Islamic faith rejects our God and believes that the state must mandate the worship of their own god, Allah." Again, both assertions are wildly incorrect.[10] Or consider an outspoken legislator in my home state of Oklahoma. Representative John Bennett from Sallisaw repeatedly grabbed local headlines with his frequent attacks on Islam. In 2014 his deplorable words drew national attention when he identified Islam as a "cancer that has to be cut out from our midst" and advocated closing all the mosques.[11] The list of local, state, and national politicians spouting anti-Islamic rhetoric goes on and on, as any Internet search will quickly demonstrate. It remains a mystery how such hostility toward Islam and Muslims can be squared with the cherished values of religious freedom and the clear mandate in Article 6 of the U.S. Constitution: "No religious test shall ever be required as a qualification to any office or public trust under the United States."

Scores of Christian leaders with television ministries or high visibility, such as Franklin Graham, the son of the late Billy Graham, the legendary evangelist, regularly denounce Islam. In the aftermath of the 9/11 attacks, Franklin Graham called Islam "wicked and evil." He decried the Qur'an for instructing Muslims to kill non-Muslims, adding, "I don't believe this is a wonderful, peaceful religion."[12] As Graham has traveled and spoken in Europe and Africa over many years, he has continually spurred controversy and opposition for his criticism of Islam.

The list of anti-Islamic preachers is long. The Rev. Jerry Vines, former president of the Southern Baptist Convention (SBC) and longtime pastor of First Baptist Church in Jacksonville, Florida, is a prime example. In a widely publicized speech to several thousand gathered for the Pastors' Conference prior to the annual SBC Convention in St. Louis in 2002, Vines declared the following:

> Pluralists would have us to believe that Islam is just as good as Christianity, but I'm here to tell you, ladies and gentlemen, that Islam is not just as good as Christianity. Islam was founded by Muhammad, a demon-possessed pedophile who had 12 wives. . . . And I will tell you Allah is not Jehovah either. Jehovah's not going to turn you into a terrorist that'll try to bomb people and take the lives of thousands and thousands of people.[13]

Jerry Vines is one of many Protestant leaders who identify as evangelicals and denounce Islam and Muslims harshly. The most prominent and influential clergy with national audiences include the Rev. Pat Robertson, Pastor John Hagee, the Rev. Robert Jeffress, and the Rev. Jerry Falwell Jr.[14] If one tunes in religious broadcasting on television or does an Internet search linking any of these names with Islam, it won't take long before the vitriol directed at Islam and Muslims is manifest.

The Rev. Rod Parsley, senior pastor of the World Harvest Church in Columbus, Ohio, has a large weekly national television audience. He's well known for his diatribes against the media, the judiciary, and homosexuality. His written and verbal pronouncements related to Islam are as inaccurate as they are incendiary. In his book *Silent No More: Bringing Moral Clarity to America . . . While Freedom Still Rings,* Parsley includes a chapter titled "Islam: The Deception of Allah." Assuming the mantle of a knowledgeable teacher, he refers to this chapter as a course in Islam 101. Parsley repeatedly declares that Allah is a "demon spirit" and mocks the Five Pillars of Islam. He ridicules Muslims and asserts that the real goal Muslims seek is nothing less than world domination. While Parsley weaves a great deal of political advocacy into his sermons, his pronouncements related to Muslims and Islam—like those of many other Protestant evangelicals—appear to be driven by a narrow fundamentalist theology. He may be ignorant or uninformed, but he is never in doubt.[15]

A more curious but profoundly disturbing and influential critique of Muhammad and Islam came from Pope Benedict XVI not long after he was elevated to be the most visible representative of Christianity in the world. In a broadly disseminated prepared speech at the University of Regensburg in Germany in September 2006, the pontiff cited a fourteenth-century Byzantine emperor's disdainful comments about Muhammad: "Show me just what Muhammad brought that was new, and there you will find things only evil and inhuman, such as his command to spread by the sword the faith he preached."[16]

The way by which Pope Benedict XVI quoted this critique of Muhammad was widely interpreted as an endorsement of a dominant view espoused by Western European Christians for many centuries. The international response of Muslims and many Christians was swift and unambiguous. Rather than simply decry the bias and bigotry manifest in the kinds of pronouncements by politicians and preachers noted above, this time thoughtful Muslim leaders endeavored to use the controversy for a teachable moment.

Constructive Religious and Pragmatic Responses to Islamophobia

Thirty-eight prominent Muslim leaders responded to Pope Benedict XVI's speech by cosigning a letter to him one month after the controversy erupted. Their initiative was much appreciated as a constructive act. It launched a hopeful movement. One year later, 138 Muslim leaders—well known Muftis (Islamic judges), academics, intellectuals, and government officials—released a statement in order to promote constructive relationships in the aftermath of the pope's speech. The letter, "A Common Word between Us and You," expressed these foundational convictions upon which Christian-Muslim relations should be built:

> Muslims and Christians together make up well over half the world's population. Without peace and justice between these two religious communities, there can be no meaningful peace in the world. The future of the world depends on peace between Muslims and Christians. . . . The basis for this peace and understanding already exists. It is part of the very foundational principles of both faiths: love of the One God, and love of the neighbor. These principles are found over and over again in the sacred texts of Islam and Christianity. . . . With the terrible weaponry of the modern world, with Muslims and Christians intertwined everywhere as never before, no side can unilaterally win a conflict between more than half the world's inhabitants. Thus our common future is at stake. The very survival of the world itself is perhaps at stake.[17]

This effort effectively mirrored the inclusive vision exemplified by the pontiff's predecessor, Pope John Paul II. We will return to John Paul II and the positive interfaith initiatives in the Roman Catholic Church after Vatican II in chapter 5 below. Following the release of "A Common Word," Christian leaders and scholars around the world publicly responded approvingly to the Muslim initiative. In the U.S., more than three hundred Christian leaders visibly endorsed a letter published as a full-page advertisement in the *New York Times* on November 18, 2007, with this title: "Loving God and Neighbor Together: A Christian Response to a Common Word between You and Us." The open letter affirms vital ways Christians and Muslims contribute to world peace. It also confirms the love for God and love toward one's neighbors as foundational teachings at the heart of both religions. The statement concludes with a pledge to support Christian-Muslim dialogue at every level.

Both "A Common Word" and "Loving God and Neighbor Together" appeal to theological and pragmatic reasons for charting a better way forward into a precarious future. Whether or not one is personally religious, the future requires better understanding and cooperation between adherents of the world's two largest religions. As the declaration above puts it succinctly, "Our common future is at stake. The very survival of the world itself is perhaps at stake." This strong warning underscores the precarious context articulated above. In the first quarter of the twenty-first century, we are in uncharted territory. Danger lurks at every turn as even small numbers of people are capable of doing great harm, and numerous flashpoints are evident in our all too quarrelsome human family. To make matters much worse, influential, religious, and political zealots and opportunists continue to fan the flames of fear, mistrust, and antipathy.

The challenges we face today are local as well as national and global. In the United States today, every city of 100,000 or more is literally a microcosm of the world. You'll find every type of Christian, Jew, Hindu, Muslim, Buddhist, Taoist, practitioner of Shinto, along with Native Americans, pagans, agnostics, atheists, and so on. Near the end of the semester in my classes on comparative religion, I have students go out in groups of three to find and interview people who self-identify as adherents within one of the religions (besides Christianity) we have studied. Some are puzzled as to where to look for Hindus, Muslims, Buddhists, Zoroastrians, or others to interview. I tell them to figure it out, and they do. When they open their eyes, they find Buddhists running Chinese restaurants and students of various backgrounds in their dorms, or they think to contact the mosque and ask to come to visit. Inevitably, several groups will be invited into the homes of a Muslim, Buddhist, or Hindu family. When the groups come back to present 20–25-minute reports on what they've learned, similar things happen every semester. They discover the same mixes of believers—some devout, some marginal—as they know exist within their own religious communities. They discover human beings with families who have the same hopes, dreams, and concerns as most people. Many have more challenges because they are in minority religious communities in a society predisposed to accommodate Christian traditions predominately. Often the Muslims they interview share concerns about the hostility and mistreatment they and their friends sometimes experience in the otherwise mundane course of daily events. The whole process is eye-opening for the class as they discover that Norman, Oklahoma, is literally teeming with religious diversity. The whole world is right here. They begin to realize that religious pluralism will be the reality of their world whether they enter some form of business, pursue a medical career, get actively involved with the PTA, or take part in almost any type of community activity.

Both "A Common Word" and "Loving God and Neighbor Together" reflect the awareness of our common humanity that the celebrated scholar and churchman Wilfred Cantwell Smith envisioned well over half a century ago. Smith, a university professor at Harvard, was a prolific historian of religion with specialization in Islamic studies. He was also an ordained minister in the United Church of Canada. In a 1959 essay on methodology in the comparative study of religion, Smith foresaw the way honest educational efforts could and should merge with the priorities of churches in the decades ahead:

> The traditional form of Western scholarship . . . was that of an impersonal presentation of an "it." The first great innovation in recent times has been the personalization of the faiths observed, so that one finds a discussion of a "they." Presently, the observer becomes personally involved, so that

the situation is one of a "we" talking about a "they." The next step is a dialogue, where "we" talk to "you." The culmination of the process is when "we all" are talking *with* each other about "us."[18]

Biblical Mandates to Guide Christians Engaging with Muslims

Shortly after I began doctoral study in comparative religion, I had the good fortune of developing a friendship with the dean of Harvard Divinity School, Krister Stendahl. He was a world-renowned New Testament scholar and an active leader in the Lutheran Church. Some years later, after he retired from his academic post, he returned to his native Sweden to serve as the Lutheran bishop in Stockholm. Stendahl was particularly pleased that I, as an ordained Baptist minister, was pursuing a doctorate in comparative religion with specialization in Islamic studies and Jewish-Christian-Muslim relations. I shared details about my paternal Jewish grandfather and the large portion of my extended family being Jewish. We talked about my academic and personal fascination with theological options to understand Christian particularity and religious pluralism. He strongly agreed with my conviction that the newly emerging Christian-Muslim dialogue initiatives in the Vatican and World Council of Churches could be increasingly important in coming years. Stendahl also expressed concern for how few Christians were serious students of Islam.

During my first year of doctoral work, Dean Stendahl gave me the great gift of affirmation both for my commitment to serious academic study of world religions and for my sense of Christian vocation focused on a teaching ministry. On one vividly memorable day, Stendahl articulated why he was so supportive and affirming. He said, "You are pursuing a path that more and more people of faith must pursue if Christians are going to be true to the biblical mandates we claim." When I asked for clarification, he provided a minilecture (or sermon, really) on the three biblical mandates to guide interfaith relationships (and all other types of relationships, too). I share with you the simple, straightforward, and compelling biblical guidance he shared with me that day.

First, the ninth of the Ten Commandments states clearly, "You shall not bear false witness against your neighbor" (Exodus 20:16). How, Stendahl asked, is it possible to avoid speaking unfairly, deceptively, unjustly, or in a harmful prejudicial way about one's neighbor when you don't know your neighbor or what she or he believes? We must always seek to know and understand our neighbors accurately and fairly, whether or not we agree with them on a given issue. Fair and honest study of Islam is a step in the right direction of not bearing false witness out of ignorance or prejudice.

Second, the Gospel of Matthew recounts a riveting encounter between Jesus and a lawyer who poses a question in order to test Jesus: "Teacher, which commandment in the law is the greatest?" Jesus responded, saying:

> "You shall love the Lord your God with all your heart, and with all your soul, and with all your mind." [Deuteronomy 6:5] This is the greatest and first commandment. And a second is like it: "You shall love your neighbor as yourself." [Leviticus 19:18] On these two commandments hang all the law and the prophets. (Matthew 22:36–40)

The third foundational biblical mandate comes from the apostle Paul. Stendahl was an expert on Paul, having written a highly acclaimed book titled *Paul among the Jews and Gentiles*. He pointed me to the passage in Paul's Letter to the Romans where he articulates the marks of a true Christian:

> Live in harmony with one another; do not be haughty, but associate with the lowly; do not claim to be wiser than you are. Do not repay anyone evil for evil, but take thought for what is noble in the sight of all. If it is possible, so far as it depends on you, live peaceably with all. (Romans 12:16–18)

Do not bear false witness against your neighbor. Love God with all your heart, with all your soul, and with all your mind, and love your neighbor as yourself. And, insofar as is possible with you, live peaceably with all. We begin to live out these mandates by learning more about what is most important for our Muslim neighbors and why the leaders who put forward "A Common Word" and "Loving God and Neighbor Together" could confidently acknowledge how these two world religions share strong foundational truths on which to build healthy and cooperative relationships in the twenty-first century.

Questions for Discussion

1. When and where have politicians and/or religious leaders in your area focused on threats posed by Islam? Have you witnessed someone question or challenge the leader's assertions? What results have you seen from situations where there is a passive response or where the assertions are questioned?

2. Why do you think Muslims and Christians, whose religions teach them to live at peace, fail so often to do so, especially in regard to one another?

3. The open letter from Muslim leaders titled "A Common Word between Us and You" refers to the foundation principles of "love of the One God, and love of the neighbor" preached by both Christianity and Islam. As a Christian, what do you consider your obligations to the Muslim neighbors in your community?

4. Have you heard someone bear false witness against or attack the Muslim neighbors in person or via email/social media where you live? What strategies for responding to this situation do you think Christians and others of goodwill should adopt?

Chapter Two

The Five Pillars

Keys to Understanding Islam

If I went back to college today, I think I would prob-
ably major in comparative religion, because that's how
integrated it is in everything that we are working on and
deciding and thinking about in life today.
                    Secretary of State John Kerry, August 7, 2013

The Five Pillars of Islam are the basic ritual devotional duties
expected of all faithful Muslims. While many non-Muslims
today know something of these requirements for praying five times
a day in the direction of Mecca, fasting during the month of Ramadan, or making the annual pilgrimage (Hajj) to Mecca, far fewer
understand what these actions are intended to accomplish and how
they interrelate with the central teachings of Islam. In fact, the Five
Pillars provide a clear lens through which the heart of Islam can
be seen. At the same time, they provide powerful and instructive
points of connection with Christians and other people of faith. The
process of demystifying the Five Pillars reveals striking similarities
linking the major religions that have stood the test of time.

A Brief Arabic Lesson

Before describing the pillars, what they entail, and how they work,
we first need to clarify the meaning of the terms *Islam* and *Muslim*.

A short Arabic lesson is instructive. Arabic, like Hebrew, is a Semitic language. Most words are derived from three consonantal roots. At a basic level, the three consonants in a particular order convey a general idea. For example, the consonants *k-t-b* broadly convey the notion of writing. By adding vowels, prefixes, suffixes, and infixes (additional consonants in the middle of the three basic consonants), different nouns, verbal forms, and so on, are created. Thus *kataba* is the third-person singular (masculine) meaning "he wrote." *Katabat* is the third-person singular (feminine) meaning "she wrote." A *kitab* is a book (a document that includes writing). A *maktab* is an office (a place where writing occurs). A *maktabah* is a library (a place where many books are present). You can see the basic consonants *k-t-b* in each of the words and how the idea of writing is directly connected to the different terms.

Salam is the Arabic word for "peace." It is employed in the most common greeting: "*Salam alaykum*" (Peace unto you). The root consonants are *s-l-m*. The basic meaning conveys both "submission to God" and "peace," the connection being that submission to God's will brings the highest form of peace. In Hebrew the equivalent for *salam* is *shalom* (like Arabic, Hebrew is a Semitic language, meaning that the two are similar to one another). The well-known Hebrew term *shalom* means "peace" and also connotes the notion of wholeness and well-being. People speaking Hebrew greet one another with *shalom*, a greeting of "peace," just as Arabic-speaking people do with *salam*.

In addition to *salam*, two other central terms are derived from the consonantal root *s-l-m*: Islam and Muslim. Islam literally means "the religion of those who submit to the will of God; the religion of peace." The meaning of the term Muslim is "one who seeks to submit to the will of God." The connection to "peace" is obvious: doing God's will brings peace. The meaning of "Islam" and "Muslim" centers on the importance of knowing and doing the will of God, behavior that will bring peace. Jews and Christians can readily relate to these theological affirmations. However, the proposition immediately raises crucial questions about God and how exactly humans are to discern God's will. The Five Pillars provide the framework that answers these questions and, at the same time, clarify the fundamental structure and world-view of Islam.[1]

Confession of Faith

The confession of faith (*shahadah* in Arabic), the first pillar of Islam, is simple and straightforward: "There is no god but God, and Muhammad is the messenger of God." These thirteen words literally roll off the tongue in Arabic: *La ilaha illa llah wa Muhammad rasul Allah.* These are traditionally the first words whispered into the ears of newborns and the last words conveyed to Muslims as death approaches. Muslims repeat this confession of faith every day. There are good reasons for these practices. The words are pregnant with meaning when one understands what the words convey.

The first half of the affirmation is the single most important truth for Muslims: There is no god but God. Islam is a radical monotheism. God is the source of all creation. Nothing has ever existed or exists now that God did not create and sustain. God is one. Nothing can or ever should be compared or equated with God. Islam flatly rejects any form of polytheism or cosmic dualism. There is no god but God. One of the most dangerous sins or human transgressions is "associating something with God" (*shirk* in Arabic). God is the Creator, Sustainer, and ultimate Judge of all creation. The monotheism expressed in these affirmations rings true for Jews and Christians as well. This is not at all surprising since Islam understands itself as the same religion revealed through prophets that produced both Judaism and Christianity. When Muslims talk about God, they are talking about the God of the Bible.

For Muslims, the one and only true God they worship is the God of Adam and Eve, Noah, Abraham, Isaac and Ishmael, Jacob, Moses, David and Solomon, John the Baptist, and Jesus. Each of these prominent biblical figures is revered as prophets or messengers of God in the Qur'an. Moses, for instance, is mentioned almost 200 times in the Qur'an; Abraham more than 100 times; and Jesus more than 90 times. Again, there is no ambiguity for

Muslims: Jews, Christians, and Muslims worship the same God. Allah is the Arabic word for God. While many non-Muslims in the West confidently insist that Allah is a different god, they are missing a key point. Allah is simply the Arabic word for God, the God of the Bible. There are approximately 15 million Arabic-speaking Christians in the Middle East today. When Middle Eastern Christians sing hymns or pray in Arabic, they sing and pray to Allah.[2]

On many occasions, I've been on television programs or in public forums where another Christian clergy argues that Allah is not the same as the God of the Bible. The most common argument is based on the traditional Christian affirmation of Jesus as the incarnation of God. If you don't include the divinity of Jesus in your understanding of God, the argument goes, you are talking about a different God. While it is certainly true that traditional Trinitarian formulations of divinity are distinctly different from the radical monotheism of Islam, they are also distinctly different from traditional Jewish understandings of God. I've yet to meet a serious Christian minister (or layperson) who would claim that Jews and Christians were not talking about the same God, the God of the Bible.

The clarifying issue is this: While Christians and Muslims are talking about the same God, they have different understandings about God. This is not particularly shocking since Christians have a wide variety of understandings about God. In fact, with a little self-reflection most people will acknowledge that their own perceptions about God have changed over time. Few people I've known still think of God as they did when they were five or six years old. Ask members of any Christian congregation to say what they mean by the word "God," and you'll receive surprisingly different answers. Upon reflection, it is not too surprising that human beings are far from united when trying to comprehend and describe a perceived reality encompassed by the term God.

What is really going on when Western Christians assert that Muslims worship a false god or worse? This is a tactic, a ploy to drive a deep wedge between Jews and Christians on the one hand, and Muslims on the other. There is a good reason why Jews, Christians, and Muslims are all called "the children of

Abraham": all three revere Abraham as their founding figure who rejected idols and followed the call of the one, true God. Different conceptions of the divine and how people in each of these communities of faith affirm ways God reveals God's will can be a very fruitful focus for intentional interfaith dialogue, a subject to which we will return in the last two chapters.

The first half of the confession of faith is clear. There is only one God, the Creator, Sustainer, and ultimate Judge. The notion of God as creator and final judge are central themes in the Bible and the Qur'an. The middle attribute—God as sustainer of creation—calls for closer examination. Islam asserts that God is right now actively engaged in sustaining creation, holding it all together. A striking image of God's intimate connection to each of us is found in Qur'an 50:16: "God is closer to you than your jugular vein." The God of all creation is also intimately bound up with everything and everyone from moment to moment—a claim with which Jews and Christians would certainly agree.

Here is the key to understanding the basic structure of Islam. Islam insists that we exist only because God created us and is this very moment sustaining us. One day we will be accountable to our creator. If you accept these fundamental truths, then the most urgent questions you should be asking are the following: What does my creator require of me? What will I be accountable for on the day of judgment? With eternity hanging in the balance, all else pales by comparison. The answer to these vital questions is lodged in the second part of the confession of faith: ". . . and Muhammad is the messenger of God." In other words, God has not left us alone to guess about what God expects or requires of us. God has revealed what humans need to know through many prophets and messengers. For Muslims, Islam is not a religion that began when Muhammad received his first revelation in the year 610 CE. Rather, it is the one true religion that God has revealed through many prophets and messengers. What we call Judaism and Christianity are understood by Muslims to be true religions that are derived from the prophetic revelations delivered through Abraham, Moses, Jesus, and others. The Qur'an repeatedly refers to Jews and Christians (and some others) as "People of the Book." Islam understands itself as the same religion as Judaism and Christianity. It is the one true religion.

An obvious question arises immediately: Why are these religious traditions distinctly different at many points if they are the same religion? Muslims begin to answer this question by insisting that the fault does not lie with the prophets, all of whom brought the same message from God. The problems begin, rather, with those who received and preserved (or failed to preserve accurately) their respective revelations.

The case related to Jesus is the most obvious and relevant for this book. Jesus is greatly loved and honored by Muslims. He is one of God's greatest prophets and messengers. The Qur'an affirms the virgin birth of Jesus. Like Adam, he is the only person born not by human procreation but by the divine decree: "Jesus is like unto Adam for God created him from dust and said 'Be!' And he was" (Qur'an 3:59).[3] The serious problem arose with those who came after Jesus. His miracles and healing ministries led some to claim that he was God. Muslims insist that no prophet would ever claim divine status. There is no god but God. Period. Muslims view the New Testament as containing a great deal of God's truth revealed through Jesus but also containing serious errors—most notably anything suggesting that Jesus was the incarnation of God. Different understandings about Jesus and the ways God's will is made known through revelation are another valuable focus for interfaith dialogue.

God has repeatedly sent prophets to all nations, but in ways large and small, the revelations have been altered or confused by followers. Islam teaches that God has revealed what human beings need to know one last time through the prophet Muhammad. This time, the revelation has been captured in its purity and preserved in the Qur'an. There will be no more revelations or prophets (Qur'an 33:40). According to Islam, the Qur'an is the final testament. The Qur'an, which is a little shorter than the 27 books comprising the New Testament, is understood as God's words. Muhammad was the vehicle, the messenger who received the revelations via the angel Gabriel and then uttered God's words. He was illiterate, unable to read or write. But the words were memorized, written down by others, and collected in the written form we have today less than 15 years after Muhammad died in 632 CE.

The Qur'an then forms the foundation for answering the key questions identified above: What does God require of me? What will I be accountable for on the day of judgment? The key point to grasp: In the first pillar of Islam, Muslims affirm that the One True God—the Creator and Sustainer of all creation—has revealed through prophets and messengers what human beings need to know to live a faithful life and be found worthy on the day of judgment. God's revelation contained foremost in the Qur'an but also in the sayings and example of the final prophet, Muhammad, establishes the foundation and framework for living a life in accordance with God's will.

Because they believe that all people are created with an inherent awareness of God, Muslims believe that atheism does not come naturally to humans. Yet more puzzling than nonbelievers are those who ostensibly believe in God yet continuously fail to seek out and do the will of God. With an eternity in heaven or hell in the balance, why would anyone not seek to know and follow the will of God? What prevents many people from doing what they inherently know and have been taught they should be doing? Every religious tradition includes a version of this issue— the human predicament—at the very heart of the tradition.

The nature of the human predicament in the biblical tradition surfaces in the third chapter of Genesis. In the story of the "fall," human beings disobey their creator and by their sin are separated from the idyllic life in the garden of Eden and their intimate relationship with God. The development of biblical Judaism centers on laws to guide the people of Israel and ritual sacrifices to atone for sinful behavior. Human sin continues to be the fundamental human predicament in the Christian tradition, but the remedy centers on different ways Christians have interpreted the once-for-all sacrificial death of Jesus, which enables reconciliation between God and humans.

Islam, too, recognizes that human beings are sinful, selfish, and prideful. But sin is not the fundamental obstacle or human predicament. Rather, the problem in Islam is that human beings are *forgetful*. In brief, here are the presuppositions in place: (1) human beings are born with a knowledge of God, and this awareness is reinforced by the natural world; (2) God created us and is literally sustaining our existence at this very moment; (3) we will be accountable to our creator on the day of judgment; and (4) God has revealed what humans need to know and do by repeatedly sending prophets and messengers, the last of whom is the prophet Muhammad. With one's eternal destiny hanging in the balance, all other earthly concerns and priorities pale by comparison. Human beings should continually seek to know and do God's will. But human beings are forgetful, easily distracted by pride, selfishness, the allure of money or power or possessions. On a given day or in a given moment, it is all too easy to be caught up in pursuit of whatever "things" we believe will make us happy or admired or satisfied. It is all too easy to allow temporal desires to distract from what ultimately matters. It is all too easy to lose track or forget that our very existence depends upon the God who created and sustains us, the God to whom we will be accountable in the end.

The vital importance of the Five Pillars now comes sharply into focus. Human beings need to be constantly reminded to stay focused on what matters most. From the first words uttered in one's ears until the last thing one hears before death—and every day in between—Muslims insist that we need to affirm "There is no god but God, and Muhammad is the messenger of God." The four other pillars rest on this same foundation as constant reminders of who God is and what God expects of us during our time on this earth. These pillars, together with the continual affirmation of faith, provide the foundational discipline that people need both to remember what matters most and then to structure their lives accordingly.

Five Daily Prayers

Five times every day, Muslims are expected to stop what they are doing, go through a short ritual cleansing, face in the direction of the Ka'bah in Mecca, and pray. Worshipers align themselves in straight lines and go through the same series of prostrations in unison, symbolizing the equality of all people before God. During these prescribed prayers (*salat* in Arabic), Muslims recite verses from the Qur'an as they meditate on God's words. While Arabic is not the first language of the large majority of Muslims worldwide, everyone learns or memorizes verses in Arabic to recite during the ritual prayers. Muslims can and do pray to God for guidance, restoration of health for a loved one, and the like. But the five daily prayers are reminders at set times—dawn, midmorning, noon, late afternoon, and evening—so one doesn't lose focus on the fundamental truths of human existence and the centrality of obedience to God, the very source of one's existence.

The origin of the five daily prayers comes from an extraordinary experience in the life of Muhammad. The event, called "Night Journey," is connected to the opening verse in chapter 17, The Night Journey:

> Glory be to God Who carried His servant by night from the Sacred Mosque to the Furthest Mosque, whose precincts We blessed, that We might show him some of Our signs. Surely He is the Hearer, the Seer. (Qur'an 17:1, auth. trans.)

In the Hadith (authoritative reports about the sayings and actions of Muhammad that we will explore in chapter 4), Muhammad explained what happened in detail. He was transported mystically by night from Mecca to Jerusalem, where he prayed with the prophets of old (Abraham, Moses, and Jesus) at the mosque "furthest out" (*masjid al-aqsa* in Arabic). The site is commemorated by the Al-Aqsa mosque, a beautiful mosque which today stands on what Muslims call the Noble Sanctuary—the Temple Mount area, the site of the Temple first planned and built by Kings David and Solomon. After praying with the prophets—an act that Muslims view as further validation of their understanding of Islam as the continuation of the religions now called Judaism and Christianity—Muhammad ascended to heaven on a white horse for a vision of Paradise and an encounter with God. He ascended from a large outcropping of rock that tradition claims is Mount Moriah, the spot where Abraham was to sacrifice Isaac in Genesis 22. The Dome of the Rock, still one of the most recognizable features of the modern city of Jerusalem, commemorates this event.

In the story Muhammad rises up to the seventh heaven and encounters God. In his understandable zeal Muhammad promises God that his people will pray fifty times a day. As he is returning to the earthly realm, Muhammad encounters Moses, who tells the younger prophet that his people will not be able to bear the burden of fifty prayers. So, in a story reminiscent of Abraham negotiating with God before the destruction of Sodom and Gomorrah (Genesis 18), Muhammad returns several times to God, and eventually they agree on five daily prayers. From this story we can see that the second pillar is rooted in a promise Muhammad made to God and is linked to biblical traditions that Jews and Christians also share.

Fasting during the Month of Ramadan

The third pillar is the fast (*sawm* in Arabic) during the sacred month of Ramadan. Muslims are expected to refrain from food, drink, smoking, sexual relations with one's spouse—things that are physically pleasurable—during the daylight hours throughout this month. Muslims follow a lunar calendar. Each month is 29 or 30 days, and the entire year is approximately 11 days shorter than the solar calendar of 365 or 366 days. Thus the month of Ramadan moves by about 11 days every year in relation to the solar calendar. If, for instance, Ramadan began on May 31 of the solar calendar one year, it would begin on May 20 the following year and about May 9 the year after that. Over the course of roughly 30 years, Ramadan will move throughout the entire solar calendar. This makes a significant difference when participating in a strenuous time of self-denial during daylight hours. If you are in Egypt or Saudi Arabia or the south of India when Ramadan falls in the summer, the temperatures are well above 100 degrees, with the sun up over 14 hours each day, making the rigors of fasting exceedingly demanding. If you are in the northernmost part of Europe and the fast comes in December when the daylight hours are minimal and the temperatures cold, the fast is obviously less demanding physically. If the fast poses dangers to one's health—a pregnant or nursing mother, a small child, a person with a medical condition—the rigorous fast is not required.

There are several key points to note about the purposes for this pillar or required ritual-devotional duty. As with other pillars, the common experience of fasting emphasizes the equality of all before God. Whether one is quite wealthy and lacking for nothing in the material world, or extremely poor and having almost nothing in the material world, the pangs of hunger and thirst are experienced in common. Going without reminds the believer that whatever blessings she or he may enjoy do come from God. And, if one is blessed with food, clean water, and material possessions, the fast is a powerful reminder of the millions of people who are far less fortunate. It thereby raises the unambiguous question directly: What are you doing with the abundant blessings God has bestowed upon you? The Qur'an and Hadith are filled with admonitions about human responsibility to help people in need—the poor, the needy, the widow, and orphan.

The month of fasting also serves to strengthen ties within one's family and the community of faith as people gather daily for predawn meals and for community meals to break the fast after sunset (called Iftars). The end of Ramadan is marked by the first of the two great festivals (*eid al-fitr* in Arabic) that generally lasts three days. Typically, each family is expected to make a donation to the poor and needy to make sure everyone has food to partake in this time of celebration. In most predominantly Muslim countries, this time is marked by a three-day holiday, during which time people gather with family and friends, send best wishes to relatives, and give gifts to children.

My first direct experience of Muslims fasting came in Cairo in August of 1977. The heat and length of daylight hours were brutal. As one might imagine, normal life slowed considerably during the day. Even so, the piety and commitment required to fulfill the requirements of such self-discipline were everywhere in evidence. As a twenty-seven-year-old Protestant Christian who grew up in the U.S.—where most people fail miserably at keeping sincerely articulated New Year's resolutions for more than a week—it was instructive and powerfully provocative to observe and discuss the components and meanings attached to the fast of Ramadan with Egyptian Muslims.

Almsgiving

The fourth pillar is required almsgiving (*zakat* in Arabic). The specific details governing how, how much, and for what purposes Muslims are obliged to give of their resources vary some in the view of religious authorities and in some predominantly Islamic countries. The most common interpretation asserts that believers should contribute 2.5 percent of their overall wealth—which includes income and all of one's possessions—annually. The major schools of Islamic law developed slightly different ways of calculating the amount an individual should give and the basis for calculating a person's wealth, but the obligation is identified in the Qur'an and reinforced in the nascent community: "And observe the prayer, and give the alms, and obey the Messenger, that you may obtain mercy" (Qur'an 24:56, auth. trans.). The Qur'an includes numerous passages underscoring the obligation to assist the poor and needy, the widow and orphan, and the like. Zakat as religious duty is summed up succinctly in the second chapter of the Qur'an:

> It is not piety to turn your faces toward the east and west. Rather, piety is he who believes in God, the Last Day, the angels, the Book, and the prophets; and who gives wealth, out of love for God, to kinsfolk, orphans, the needy, the traveler, beggars, and for [the ransom of] slaves; and observes the prayer and gives the alms; and those who fulfill their oaths when they pledge them, and those who are patient in misfortune, hardship, and moments of peril. It is they who are the sincere, and it is they who are the God-fearing. (Qur'an 2:177, auth. trans.)

The basic duties of the obligatory daily prayers and almsgiving underscore two vital dimensions of obedience to God: the vertical relationship between a person and God through prayer; and the horizontal relationship with other believers as manifest by helping to meet their needs from one's resources. Strictly speaking, this is not a favor one is doing for others. Rather, it is an act of worship and obedience to God, the true source of all we have. Islamic understandings of afterlife include a judgment scene during which each person will be given a book, the record of your life. Like prayer and fasting, almsgiving is a ritual-devotional duty that Muslims should fulfill in gratitude and in obedience to the Creator, Sustainer, and ultimate Judge. Over and above the obligation of Zakat, Muslims are directed by the Qur'an and the guidance of the prophet to give often and freely to charitable causes.

In the early centuries of Islam, scholars of the Qur'an and Hadith clarified parameters for eight types of recipients of Zakat: (1) people who are poor (without the ability to provide a livelihood); (2) people who are needy, unable to meet their basic needs; (3) the people whose job is to collect Zakat; (4) recent converts or people who are sympathetic and considered likely to convert to Islam; (5) people for whom the resources will enable them to become free from slavery; (6) people who have amassed insurmountable debt by simply trying to meet basic needs; (7) people who are fighting for a righteous cause; and (8) travelers who need assistance to reach their destination. Zakat cannot be given to close family members, and often discretion or anonymity is important to avoid embarrassment of recipients.

While Zakat has been very beneficial within the Muslim communities for centuries, the variations in practices and qualifying recipients have also posed challenges at times. In recent decades, for instance, some Muslim extremists have sought out Zakat contributions deceptively in support of militant groups like al-Qaida, ISIS, or Islamic Jihad. In the view of many violent extremists, they justify this by claiming that they are "striving or fighting for a righteous cause." I've heard many stories about pious Muslims who strongly opposed the violent extremism of the groups noted above, later learning that a portion of their Zakat went or may have gone to support such groups. While there are safeguards and it is possible to know a good deal about the distribution of Zakat, there are a lot of ambiguities as well. A familiar situation many in the U.S. have experienced illustrates the challenge. When pulling up to a stoplight in a major city, sometimes people will approach a car with a bucket for contributions. They often hold a sign saying something like "Feeding hungry children downtown" or "Can you help us raise money for basketball uniforms for our girls team?" In the few seconds before the light changes, many people will make a decision to pitch loose change, a dollar, or five dollars into the bucket in order to help out. But there is no easy way of knowing if the stated goal of the collection is what is being presented. You may be feeding an addiction or even giving money that will find its way to groups you would never want to support. Even so, your intention was good, and that is important.

The Pilgrimage to Mecca

The final pillar of Islam is the Hajj, the annual pilgrimage to Mecca.[4] Muslims who are physically and financially able to perform this journey and the detailed ritual components are obliged to do so at least once in their life. The five days of rituals occur during the final month of the Islamic lunar calendar. The specific events each day are connected directly to the experiences in the stories about Abraham and Muhammad that are set in specific places in and around Mecca. Pilgrims are effectively reenacting key events and connecting symbolically and spiritually with these prophets. The ritual acts begin with circumambulating the Ka'bah seven times in a counterclockwise direction and walking or running back and forth between the hills of Safa and Marwah before drinking from the well of Zamzam. This back and forth represents Hagar's desperate search for water when she and Ishmael were nearing death in the desert (Muslims, like Jews and Christians, trace their heritage back to Abraham, yet through the lineage of Ishmael, Abraham's firstborn son). Muslims identify Mecca as the location of the Genesis story (see Genesis 21:8–21).

Before beginning and throughout the Hajj, the faithful enter a special spiritual state, called *ihram*, during which they focus on

God and abstain from certain actions, such as no special adornments and no applying perfume. Men wear two seamless pieces of white cloth, a symbol of simplicity, the state of purity, and equality of all before God. Each day includes compelling symbolic acts that connect believers to other key events associated with Abraham and Muhammad. At the plain of Arafat some 12 miles from Mecca, for example, pilgrims stand from noon until sunset for prayer and meditation. This portion of the Hajj replicates the gathering at the Mount of Mercy, where Muhammad revealed the final portion of the Qur'an and gave what would be his farewell sermon. After sundown that day, the pilgrims in a mass journey about halfway back toward Mecca, where they spend the night, and gather 70 stones for a dramatic event the following day. Returning to Mina on the outskirts of Mecca, each believer throws 70 stones at one of three pillars representing Satan. In the Islamic version of the near sacrifice of Abraham's son (whom most Muslims identify as Ishmael rather than Isaac), Satan appears three times to encourage Abraham to disobey God's command. Each time, Abraham chases the devil away by throwing stones at him. Pilgrims get very animated in a frenzied reenactment of this story as they also reflect on their own internal battles with temptations that might lead them astray.[5]

The conclusion of the Hajj each year is marked by the second of the worldwide Islamic festivals, the Festival of Sacrifice (*eid al-adha* in Arabic). This event commemorates the story of Abraham's willingness to sacrifice his son in obedience to God's directive. Just before Abraham completed the sacrifice, God intervened and provided a ram to substitute as the sacrificial offering (see Genesis 22:1–14 and Qur'an 37:99–113). This annual celebration is enormous, with millions of animals sacrificed. The meat from the sacrifices is distributed in thirds: one-third for the family, one-third for relatives and close friends, and one-third for the poor and needy. The ritual sacrifices and distributions occur all over the world. In Mecca, where more than two million pilgrims have just completed the Hajj, the logistics behind processes to prepare for and complete this obligation—including shipping meat to distant lands—are massive.

This festival or celebration includes special prayers in the mosques, where men, women, and children normally dress in their nicest clothes. Following prayers, Muslims exchange greetings and visits with one another and often exchange gifts. The celebration or holiday continues for three days. While the Hajj is a requirement for all Muslims, many other lesser forms of pilgrimage are practiced as well.[6]

Relating Christian Belief and Practice to the Five Pillars of Islam

Demystifying the meanings and purposes of these essential ritual-devotional duties in Islam reveals multiple points of commonality as well as differences between practicing Christians and Muslims. A closer look at the common affirmations, obligations, and practices is not only highly instructive; it also provides valuable bases for Christian-Muslim dialogue and cooperation, a major focus of chapters 5 and 6, respectively.

The first pillar, the Shahadah or declaration of faith, establishes the foundation in Islam. A comparable truth undergirds Judaism and Christianity. All three religious traditions revere Abraham as the pivotal figure who recognized and put his trust in the One True God. Jews and Christians traditionally have no difficulty affirming the monotheism that Muslims repeatedly declare: "There is no god but God." God is the source of creation and the One to whom we will all be accountable on the day of judgment.

The second part of the Shahadah, ". . . and Muhammad is the messenger of God," has not been traditionally affirmed by Christians or Jews. When we go deeper and reflect on what is being communicated by Muslims, as we have done above, striking points of agreement become visible. To declare Muhammad as God's final prophet and messenger is to affirm the centrality of revelation. God has revealed what humans need to know through many prophets and messengers. Jesus' parable of the Rich Man and Lazarus underscores the importance of God's prophets: "If they do not listen to Moses and the prophets, neither will they be convinced even if someone rises from the dead" (Luke 16:19–31).

Christians and Muslims agree that God has revealed what humans need to know and do through prophets. The point of disagreement surfaces around understandings of God's consummate revelation. For Muslims, it comes through the final prophet, Muhammad, and is contained in the Qur'an. The Qur'an is understood to literally be God's word. For Christians, God's fullest revelation comes in the person of Jesus. Christians traditionally understand Jesus as divine, the incarnation of God. Jesus, not the Bible, is the Word of God: "And the Word became flesh and lived among us, and we have seen his glory, the glory as of a father's only son, full of grace and truth" (John 1:14). The New Testament bears witness to what God has done in and through Jesus' life, death, and resurrection. Christians and Muslims agree that God has revealed what humans need to know and do, but they disagree on the way God's final revelation has come to humankind.

It is readily apparent that Christians and Muslims share the conviction that daily communing with God through prayer is efficacious. For Muslims, it is an obligatory practice and provides the discipline that people need to stay on the straight path. Prayer and daily focus on God for Christians takes many forms in different Christian communions. Many believers incorporate daily prayers or devotional time in private. Individual and corporate prayers are part of worship weekly or more frequently in some churches. Roman Catholics conduct Mass every day. Monks and nuns historically devote much of their lives to prayer and worship.

The primary point of Salat is to stop whatever one is doing five times a day to remember God as the Creator, Sustainer, and Judge of one's life. This discipline helps keep priorities in order by remembering what God expects of humans and seeking to act accordingly. Some Sufis, the mystics of Islam, advocate moving beyond the five daily prayers to constantly remember God in everything at all times. There is a clear parallel in the New Testament when the apostle Paul famously exhorts followers of Christ in his earliest recorded letter: "Rejoice always, pray without ceasing, give thanks in all circumstances; for this is the will of God in Christ Jesus for you" (1 Thessalonians 5:16–18).

While there is no obvious reason for Christians to object or find fault with the Muslim requirement of Salat, I've met many who criticize the prayers as too ritualistic and not spontaneous. After I explain the reasons for the five daily prayers and point out that Muslims pray spontaneously for all kinds of reasons as well, I then offer this suggestion: Experiment for a month with the discipline of stopping whatever you are doing at the same five designated times each day so you can pray. The first time for prayer, by the way, is around 5:00 a.m. Several who have accepted the challenge have decided within a few days that God doesn't really need to hear from them at 5:00 a.m. each day. Like me, many also come away with a newfound appreciation and respect for the discipline it takes to interrupt one's life five times a day to focus on God through prayer.

A demanding month of fasting is an unambiguously prominent feature of Muslim life. Fasting is a common feature in all the major religions as people worldwide have found a meaningful connection between physical self-denial and spiritual insight or power. Physical self-denial is far more important in the biblical tradition—and in the historic branches of Judaism and Christianity—than I and most Protestants in America were taught.

In the Jewish tradition, fasting has been both an individual practice and a requirement for the whole community of faith. In the books of Exodus, Numbers, Deuteronomy, 1 and 2 Samuel, and Joel, for example, fasting is prescribed when danger threatened or as a sign of mourning when a calamity befell the nation or when a prophet was preparing to receive a revelation. The one major, obligatory fast occurs on the most sacred day in the annual Jewish calendar: Yom Kippur, the Day of Atonement.

It wasn't until I began studying world religions and experienced Ramadan in Egypt in August of 1977 that my eyes began to see truths within my own religious tradition. For the first time, I began to grasp what Catholic and Orthodox Christians had understood all along: that because fasting is a frequent companion to prayer in the life and message of Jesus, the two should find a home together in our lives as well.[7] In a lengthy passage in Mark's Gospel, Jesus heals a boy with an unclean spirit after the disciples had been unable to do so. When the disciples later ask Jesus why they could not exorcise the spirit, Jesus replies, "This kind can only come out through prayer and fasting" (Mark 9:14–29).[8]

My experiences studying Islam and other religions that have stood the test of time mirrors the benefits Barbara Brown Taylor articulates beautifully in *Holy Envy: Finding God in the Faith of Others*.[9] The study of Islamic pillars of prayer and fasting are clear examples. These experiences have not only produced a deep appreciation for these Muslim spiritual disciplines, they have also opened my eyes to underappreciated elements of my own religious tradition.

The requirement for charitable giving is obviously present in all three Abrahamic traditions. In the Hebrew Bible, the principle of giving or setting aside 10 percent (a tithe) is well established (see Leviticus 27:30; Numbers 18:26; Deuteronomy 14:22–23; 2 Chronicles 31:5; and Malachi 3:9–10). Many Christians have followed this rule of 10 percent as a foundational guide for giving of their annual income. Like Muslims, many Christians give far more than the respective amounts to religious and charitable causes. In both religions, the principles are the same. The resources that people enjoy are made possible by blessings from God. In recognition of the abundance we enjoy and to help those in need, people of faith should give generously.

Islam explicitly includes social obligations as an essential component of religious practice. The Qur'an repeatedly emphasizes the obligation to respond generously to the needs of the poor, the widow, and the orphan. It figures prominently in passages about the day of judgment. Similarly, how one responds to the visible needs of others is the basis for judgment in the aforementioned parable of the Rich Man and Lazarus, as well as the other well-known teaching of Jesus on the Judgment of the Nations (Matthew 25:31–46). It is likewise the central focus of the parable of the Good Samaritan (Luke 10:25–37), one of the best-known and frequently preached-upon passages in the New Testament.

Finally, some reflection on the common phenomena of pilgrimage to sacred places is also instructive. The desire to connect physically with places that are especially meaningful is universal.

We recognize this in secular life when we return to our home-towns, gather at high schools or colleges for reunions, return to places with positive memories of family vacations, and so forth. Personal connection with places associated with sacred stories happens all the time, both symbolically and literally. Think of worship services during the Christmas season. The familiar songs, lighting, and pageantry all serve to re-create the events in the "Little Town of Bethlehem," where "Shepherds Watched Their Fields" on that "Silent Night, Holy Night." Christians festively "Deck the Halls with Boughs of Holly," sing "Joy to the World" and "Away in a Manger" to celebrate Jesus' birth. There are obvious parallels during Holy Week, where the events of Palm Sunday, Maundy Thursday, and Good Friday re-create events that culminate with Easter, when sunrise services include the joyful proclamation that "Christ the Lord Is Risen Today." These dramatic rituals—like the Lord's Supper and baptism—connect people today symbolically with the most sacred stories shared by the community of faith through the ages. Making pilgrimage to sacred sites incorporates physical contact with the actual places where the events are believed to have occurred.

Each year, several hundred thousand Christian pilgrims travel to the Holy Land. While pilgrimage to sacred places is not obligatory for Christians as it is for Muslims who are physically and financially able to make the Hajj, the experiences are often profound for people in both communities who make such journeys to enrich and deepen their faith.

For many Christians living alongside Muslims, the Five Pillars of Islam are neither alien nor confusing. They find parallel practices in Christianity. However, for Christians in Europe and the West, such appreciation for common points connecting different descendants of Abraham has been rare. What accounts for these differences among Christians historically and today? In the next two chapters we will explore how these dynamics developed and significant obstacles that inhibit the kinds of constructive relationships necessary between Christians and Muslims in the volatile world of the twenty-first century.

Questions for Discussion

1. How much detail about each of the Five Pillars of Islam did you know before reading this chapter? Have you participated in an Iftar meal during Ramadan with Muslims?
2. Are Jews, Christians, and Muslims talking about and worshiping the same God? Why or why not?
3. Islam asserts that the fundamental human problem is that we have forgotten the truth about ourselves and God. In your experience, what truths do Christians most often fail to keep at the forefront of their minds?
4. Have you ever fasted for religious reasons? Did you find the experience meaningful? If so, in what ways?
5. The Five Pillars oblige Muslims to do something: worship, pray, fast, give, go. How do these obligations compare to what you understand the Bible calls Christians to do?

Chapter Three

Conflict and Cooperation

How We Got Here

> Lord, make me an instrument of Thy peace; where there
> is hatred, let me sow love.
>
> Prayer of St. Francis of Assisi

A large majority of Americans I've encountered for over four decades sincerely believe that Islam is somehow inherently violent and menacing to Christians. I've heard this view as expressed by friends, members of my extended family, people in churches and classrooms, at colleges and universities where I've lectured, and in various civic organizations where I've been a speaker. When asked, many reflexively repeat the common refrain that "Christians and Muslims (or Jews and Muslims) have been fighting for thousands of years." A few actually know that Islam as we know it began just over 1,400 and not "thousands" of years ago; most appear oblivious as they confidently repeat what they've come to believe.

These views have deep roots in Europe and the West. The rapid expansion of Islam, simplistic perceptions of the Crusades, and a long history of anti-Muslim literature in Europe have fueled the popular views for many centuries. Fear and confusion about Islam have been intensified exponentially in the past half-century by extensive media coverage of revolutions, upheavals, internal conflicts, and regional wars in several Muslim-majority countries.

While turbulence, revolutions, and wars have been frequent also in Latin America, Africa, and Asia, countries like Afghanistan, Iran, Iraq, Syria, Israel/Palestine, and Lebanon have received far more media attention in the West.[1] These dramatic, frightening images are further reinforced by the appalling behavior of emergent nonstate extremist groups like al-Qaida in Afghanistan, Iraq, Yemen, and elsewhere; the Islamic State in Syria (ISIS); and Boko Haram in Nigeria.

In the first chapter, we identified many settings where people and groups claiming inspiration from Islam have been and are perpetrating horrific acts of violence. Tragically, in some places minority Christian communities and churches have been the intentional targets of attacks by extremists. Such deplorable events effectively buttress and deepen the narratives pushed by both some Muslim extremists and many highly visible politicians, preachers, and pundits in America: the persecution or overt attacks on Christians are reflections of the larger global clash between Muslims and Christians, or Muslims on one side and Jews and Christians on the other. Many people go even further and speak generically of a "clash of civilizations," a concept that doesn't hold up to serious scrutiny but does reinforce a broader "us" versus "them" worldview.

To be sure, Christians and Muslims, at different times and in different places, have experienced periods of heightened tensions, mutual antipathy, and open hostility. Far less is known in the West about the history of cooperation and peaceful coexistence between these two communities claiming descent from their common patriarch, Abraham. In addition to a long-standing academic study of Christian-Muslim relations, I have lived and worked with Middle Eastern Christians and engaged the interfaith dynamics in various Muslim-majority lands for decades. After living in Cairo, Egypt, and traveling in neighboring countries in 1977–78 as part of my doctoral program, I have traveled throughout the region more than 35 times. Much of the work related directly to the leaders and churches of the 15–16 million indigenous Arabic-speaking Christians. The vast majority of these Christian communities trace their roots back to the first and second century. They were there long before the rise of Islam, and they have lived side by side with the Muslim majority since the seventh century CE. This reality does not square with the narrative about continuous conflict and war between Muslims and Christians. Fear, stoked by partial truths and misinformation, often trumps the reality one finds "on the ground."

If Muslims are supposed to kill Christians (and Jews), as some extremist individuals and groups claim and many Western Christian preachers and pundits assert by selectively citing passages from the Qur'an, how does one explain the continuing presence of so many millions of Christians? With the exception of Lebanon, Muslims have comprised 85–90 percent of the population throughout the region for over a thousand years. Despite times of conflict and persecution of minority communities, Middle Eastern Christians and Muslims have lived together remarkably well for centuries in Egypt, Israel/Palestine, Lebanon, Jordan, Syria, and elsewhere. Knowing more about both the positive and negative ways these diverse communities of faith have interacted not only establishes a foundational understanding of how we got to where we are in the twenty-first century; it also provides bases for hope in fashioning a more constructive future between adherents of the world's two largest and most geographically diverse religions.

Interfaith Relations in Muhammad's Lifetime and the First Centuries of Islam

Muhammad was born in Mecca in 570 CE, five and a half centuries after the time of Jesus. He grew up in the midst of religious diversity. At that time, the Arabian Peninsula was characterized by having a wide variety of local deities and practices. Amid the hodgepodge of indigenous religions, there were some monotheists as well. Like others in Mecca, Muhammad encountered Jews and Christians not only in Arabia but also through travel with caravans taking goods to neighboring lands. When Muhammad began to proclaim the words that Muslims believe God revealed to him through the angel Gabriel, the monotheism he received was understood as being in the same tradition as the biblical prophets. Although the call to worship the One True God was not entirely new, it was perceived and experienced as a direct threat to the leaders in the Quraysh, the powerful tribe that controlled Mecca.

The early revelations uttered by Muhammad challenged the economic and social status quo in several destabilizing ways. The call to worship Allah alone undermined the lucrative business that the leaders of Mecca enjoyed as they catered to the religious worldviews and ritualistic wishes of all who passed through and stayed in their important oasis town. At that time, the Ka'bah, the simple cube-shaped stone building in Mecca, housed over one hundred idols, representing different deities. The Meccan leaders were all too happy to add more or cater to all who stopped in Mecca for hospitality or religious festivals. Muhammad's message insisted that all of these deities and practices had to be abolished. Two decades later, on his farewell pilgrimage to Mecca, Muhammad purged the Ka'bah of the idols and restored this sacred structure that Muslims believe was built or restored by Abraham and Ishmael as the first house of worship to God.

In addition to the economic threat posed by Muhammad's prophetic utterances, he conveyed the socially disruptive message that all people are equal before God. All people? Men and women? Members of the Quraysh (the most powerful tribe in Mecca) and nomads? This foundational claim of equality before God was a direct affront to the deeply entrenched, male-dominated, and hierarchical tribal structure in Mecca and Arabia. A clear example came in an early revelation that flatly rejected established social norms by forbidding the accepted practice of female infanticide. While male children were highly prized in pre-Islamic Arabia, females were often seen as a burden to parents or even a source of shame. Baby girls were sometimes buried alive in the desert shortly after birth. The Qur'an warned that those who killed female infants would be exposed on the day of judgment.

> When the female infant, buried alive, is questioned—for what crime was she killed; when the scrolls are laid open; when the World on High is unveiled; when the Blazing Fire

is kindled to fierce heat; and when the Garden is brought near—Then shall each soul know what it has put forward. (Qur'an 81:8–14)

Numerous other Qur'anic passages and Hadith echo themes of equality between men and women before God and a woman's rights in marriage, divorce, and inheritance. Even slaves were declared to be equal with others before God. In a well-known story, the slave of a prominent Meccan leader embraced Islam. He was threatened with death unless he recanted his declaration of faith in Allah alone. Abu Bakr, one of Muhammad's closest friends and an early convert to Islam, saved the slave by purchasing him at a very high price. He then set him free. The former slave, Bilal, became prominent in early Islam as the first Muslim to sing out the lyrical public call to prayer after the community was established in Medina.

If Muhammad had not been a member of the ruling Quraysh tribe and under the protection of a powerful uncle, the angry leaders in Mecca would surely have eliminated him for his direct challenge to their economic well-being and the established social structures. As more people embraced Islam, the Meccan leaders did begin to impose increasingly serious and systematic persecution, including death to some who weren't protected by membership in the Quraysh. A famous episode—called the Abyssinian Affair—was directly linked to the persecution of Muslims in Mecca. It also reveals a foundational understanding of the traditional Islamic attitude and approach to followers of Jesus.

By 615, five years after Muhammad's initial call to a prophetic ministry, he sent a group of the most vulnerable to the West so they might have protection in Abyssinia (now Ethiopia). The Meccan leaders, who had a history of trade with this neighboring African land, dispatched a delegation to seek extradition of the Muslims. Their appeal to the respected Christian monarch, the Negus, was rejected, however. When the Negus and his bishops asked the Muslims about the charges against them, they offered an explanation of the religion that God had revealed to Muhammad. Upon hearing a recitation about the Virgin Mary and Jesus from the Qur'an (in what is now chapter 19), the Negus was moved to tears. He famously drew a line on the ground and declared this to be all that separated these people from followers of Jesus. He then refused to turn the Muslim refugees over to the Meccans, and he guaranteed their protection in his Christian land.

The second story concerns the three Jewish tribes living in Yathrib when Muhammad and the Muslims arrived there from Mecca in 622. Initially recruited by leaders in Yathrib to be an arbiter among contentious tribes in their city, Muhammad quickly became the temporal leader in the city now called Medina (Medina means "the city" and is short for *medinat an-nabi*, "The city of the Prophet"). He thus became the political, religious, and military leader simultaneously. While many in Medina embraced Islam, many others did not, including members of the three Jewish tribes. A practical question immediately arose: If the organizing principle for government in Medina was no longer based on powerful and traditional tribal leadership but instead centered on membership in the Islamic community, the *ummah*, what was the status of those people who didn't embrace Islam? Most immediately, what about the Jews in Medina?

Muhammad established a formal agreement between the Muslims and non-Muslims in Medina. Several early Islamic documents include versions of this "constitution" or "charter" of Medina.[2] It contains rules for diverse communities living together under the authority of Islam. Several provisions reveal the framework that Muhammad established in this constitution: in order to provide security for the community, Medina was to be free from violence and weapons; religious freedoms and security for women were guaranteed; a tax system was established to support the community's needs, especially in time of conflict with the Meccans; and a judicial system provided for peaceful resolution of disputes. The Jewish tribes were considered part of the community of believers. Jews were free to practice their religion without interference as long as they did not impede the Muslims. Jews were required to pay taxes to support the cost of war against Meccan enemies of Islam, but they and other non-Muslims were not obligated to fight in the religious wars of the Muslims.

The Constitution of Medina is consistent with the Qur'an's affirmation of previous prophets like Moses and Jesus, whose revelations are referred to as the Torah and Gospel. Jews and Christians are "People of the Book." Religious diversity is acknowledged prominently in the Qur'an as part of God's plan:

> If God had so willed, He would have created you as one community, but [He has not done so] that He may test you in what He has given you; so compete with one another in good works. To God you shall all return, and He will tell you the truth about that which you are disputing. (Qur'an 5:48)
>
> O mankind! Behold We created you from a male and female, and We made you nations and tribes that you may come to know one another. Truly the most noble of you before God are the most reverent of you. Behold God is all-Knowing, Aware. (Qur'an 49:13, auth. trans.)

These well-known dynamics between the Muslims, Christians, and Jews during Muhammad's lifetime serve as an important resource for constructive interfaith relationships throughout Islamic history. But positive relationships were not the only reality in Medina. Over a period of four years, each of the Jewish tribes was expelled from Medina amid charges of collaborating with the enemies of Islam. Details about various circumstances supporting charges of treason—particularly against the last tribe expelled and treated very harshly—are difficult to substantiate. The foundational principles, however, are clearly established under the leadership of the prophet: Jews (and Christians) living under Islamic rule have their rights and should be protected unless they are guilty of joining forces with the enemies who are attacking Islam and Muslims. When Muslims are attacked, they have the right and responsibility to fight back in self-defense and in defense of Islam. A great deal depends, of course, on who is interpreting what constitutes being attacked in such a way as to legitimize a defense according to Islamic understanding.

The long history of sizeable Jewish communities living under Muslim rule supports this basic attitude and approach of Muslims living peacefully together with the Jewish minority. Before the establishment of the modern State of Israel in 1948, there were substantial Jewish populations in Persia (Iran), Mesopotamia (Iraq), Syria/Lebanon, Palestine, Egypt, the Magreb (especially Morocco), and during five centuries of Islamic rule in Spain. As noted above, the continuing presence of much larger groups of Christians throughout lands controlled by Muslims also validates the point. Why then has the dominant view of Islam as a threat been so widely held in Europe and the West? The answers are found in the rise and rapid spread of Islam and the images of Islam popularized by Christian leaders and exceedingly influential literature in Europe over many centuries.

The Expansion of Islamic Civilization

When Muhammad died in 632 CE, the nascent community selected Abu Bakr for the new position of Caliph. The Caliph assumed all the duties of Muhammad as religious, political, social, economic, and military leader of the community. But the Caliph was not a prophet. Prophecy ended with Muhammad, and the Qur'an was complete. Abu Bakr ruled for two years, during which time the Muslims consolidated control over the Arabian Peninsula. During the ten-year reign of the next Caliph, Umar, Muslims dramatically expanded their military and political control. Umar's armies went north and then west into Palestine, and by 636 they had captured Jerusalem. They continued north into Syria, east into Mesopotamia and Persia, and west into Egypt and North Africa. Under the leadership of a North African general, Tariq ibn Zayid, the Muslims entered Spain in 711 at Gibraltar. In honor of Tariq's conquest, they named the famous site the "mountain of Tariq" (*jabal* is the Arabic term for "mountain," hence the name: *jabal* Tariq or Gibraltar).

The swift expansion continued, and by 732 CE, one hundred years after Muhammad's death, Muslims controlled North Africa and all of Spain in one direction and lands as distant as current-day Pakistan/India in the other direction. Contrary to popular opinion, the military conquests did not involve plundering everything in sight or forcing conversions at the point of a sword. There is little evidence, in fact, of forced conversions. Muslims, like Christians, know that faith cannot be imposed. The Qur'an states this cardinal tenet succinctly: "There is no coercion in religion" (2:256). In addition, the "People of the Book" were understood to be following the same religion revealed by Moses and Jesus, respectively, albeit with errors and distortions that Muslims believed the Qur'an had corrected. Though Christians are especially suspect theologically because of the doctrine of the Trinity and the assertion of Jesus' divinity, the Qur'an still affirms that salvation is possible for the People of the Book.

> Truly those who believe, and those who are Jews, and the Christians, and the Sabeans—whosoever believes in God and the Last Day and do righteous works will have their reward with their Lord. No fear will come upon them, nor will they grieve. (Qur'an 2:62 and 5:69, auth. trans.)

For most Christians living in the Fertile Crescent or North Africa during the seventh and eighth centuries, Islam was not seen as a new religion. This was consistent with the way Muslims understood and presented their religion as the continuation of the same true religion that God had revealed time and again through many prophets and messengers. It is both striking and informative that the first coherent critique of Islam—that of the well-educated Christian theologian John of Damascus (died around 750 CE)—framed Islam not so much as a false new religion, but as the perversion of a true, old one. John lived at the very center of the Islamic world. From 661 to 750 CE, Damascus was the seat of the Ummayad Caliphate. John acknowledged the key components that linked Muslims with Christians: belief in One God, creator of the universe; the messages of prophets; the virgin birth of Jesus; belief in the presence of spiritual beings like angels and demons; the coming day of judgment; the immortality of the soul; the existence of heaven and hell; the importance of good works and care for the poor, the orphan, and others with tangible needs; and so on. The major points of divergence, however, made this powerful religious movement a dangerous threat to central tenets of Christianity by denying the divinity of Jesus, denying the crucifixion and resurrection of Jesus, and rejecting the doctrine of the Trinity.[3]

If the most informed and articulate theologian of that time viewed Islam not as a different religion but as a heretical Christian movement, the "conversion" of so many Christians in the Fertile Crescent and across North Africa becomes more understandable. Many people almost certainly didn't think of themselves as converting to another religion at all. Most people were illiterate and were dependent on what religious leaders told them about the Bible and different doctrines. It is not a stretch to see how many could embrace what the successful new conquering forces proclaimed: Islam is the same but now corrected religion that they already embraced.

Christians (and Jews) living in predominantly Muslim lands were called *dhimmis*, or "protected people." They could practice their religion and normally had jurisdiction over religious matters within the community. As "protected people," they had to pay higher taxes, and Christians were not allowed to proselytize. Muslim rule in Spain is frequently cited as an example of Jews and Christians living reasonably well and even thriving as minority communities.[4]

At times and in different settings, however, life was considerably more difficult for Christians. As is true with all of human history and experience, there often exists a gap between the principles meant to guide relationships between majority and minority religions and the actual behavior of those in powerful positions. In addition to many examples of peaceful and cooperative coexistence, one can also identify times where disputes, accusations, and the behavior of ruthless people in positions of power created oppressive conditions for those in the minority.

Despite difficulties and limitations, Christians living with Muslims in territories controlled by Islamic rulers viewed Islam quite differently than Christians in Western Europe. Given the rapid military, political, and religious expansion of the Muslim-controlled lands, European Christians almost universally viewed

Islam as an impending threat. These fears had merit. Once the Christian church had grown beyond its humble beginnings and developed into an empire, no significant religious tradition or civilizational system had posed such a danger. The theological and philosophical similarities and distinctions between the two religions raised puzzling intellectual positions even as the astonishing military and political successes by Muslims presented an existential danger. By the time Pope Urban II called for the First Crusade in 1095 CE, many in Europe had been whipped into a near-hysterical frenzy. Thousands of zealous believers were ready to fight back.

The Crusades and Western Views of Islam in the Middle Ages

The Crusades were launched at the end of the eleventh century, ostensibly to recapture the Holy Land from the Muslims. Several factors, however, weighed heavily in the religious and political machinations that compelled European Christians to mount the Crusades over several centuries. In addition to the religious zeal to reclaim holy sites, the tensions between Eastern and Western Christendom in the aftermath of the great schism of 1054 played a significant role.[5] The degree of internal Christian animosity is reflected in the suffering experienced by Eastern Orthodox Christians during various onslaughts. Opening new trade routes to the east was yet another factor encouraging the massive military expeditions. The Crusades cast a long shadow over many centuries. Medieval writers were inspired by the stories of chivalry and fighting for holy causes. Predictably, the images of Islam that permeated Western Europe were consistently negative. British historian Norman Daniel has done the most extensive study of Islam in the eyes of Western Christians, focusing particularly on the twelfth through fourteenth centuries.[6] His work reveals how extensive and almost universally negative were the images of Islam in the West.

Europeans often considered Islam as a product of the devil or antichrist. Many alleged that Muhammad's followers worshiped him as a god. It was commonly believed that Muhammad had trained a white dove to sit on his shoulder as a prop to deceive followers into thinking he spoke as one inspired by God's Spirit. Another particularly demeaning popular story claimed that swine killed Muhammad while he was in the process of urinating. Such exceedingly degrading images and fictitious stories circulated throughout Europe for centuries. It is important to grasp how profoundly offensive such depictions of Muhammad have been and continue to be for Muslims. Disparaging portrayals of Muhammad as a fake, a licentious womanizer, a charlatan who made up the Qur'an or was a tool of the devil—all these strike a particularly sensitive nerve. As noted in the previous chapter, the Qur'an refers to Muhammad as "a beautiful model" (Qur'an 33:21), an exemplar of the faith, one whom Muslims seek to emulate.

Persistent demeaning attacks on the prophet by Western Christians is not only an affront; in addition, virtually all Muslims find it insolent in a way that defies comprehension. Muslims would never be critical or in any way disrespectful toward any of God's prophets. Whatever political or other conflict there may be with Christians, predominantly Christian nations, or the State of Israel, no devout Muslims would speak in a demeaning way about Moses or David or Jesus or John the Baptist. I have been in the midst of some of the most intense contemporary conflict situations, with clear sectarian divides between Christians, Muslims, and Jews—from the Iran hostage crisis of 1979–81, the ongoing Israeli-Palestinian conflict, and the multisided war in Lebanon (1975–89). I have never once heard any Muslim—including Sunni Muslim leaders of HAMAS in Gaza, Shi'ite leaders in Iran, and Hizbullah in Lebanon, for example—say anything negative about Jesus or any biblical prophet.

Several prominent, violent reactions to demeaning portrayals of Muhammad in the West reveal how deep and painful is the offense these long-standing portrayals evoke. In 1988, an international storm erupted immediately after the publication of Salman Rushdie's book *The Satanic Verses*. Most Muslims viewed the book as a thinly veiled mocking of Islam and their prophet. In 2005, an international furor erupted after a Danish newspaper, *Jyllands-Postem*, published twelve cartoons depicting Muhammad in ways that many Muslims found deeply offensive. And, on January 7, 2015, gunmen stormed the Paris offices of *Charlie Hebdo*, a satirical and self-proclaimed atheist magazine, after it published cartoons of Muhammad. Ten members of the staff were killed on that fateful day. We will discuss these and other contemporary events in more detail when examining both the positive and the challenging dynamics shaping contemporary Christian-Muslim relations in the next chapter.

Christians in Europe were rarely neutral or positive when they thought of Muslims and Islam. Dante's influential *Inferno* immortalized the prevailing sentiment in Europe with a lurid and grotesque picture of Muhammad and his son-in-law, Ali, languishing in the ninth chasm of hell, a region reserved for those whom Dante considered sowers of discord, scandal, and schism. Their gruesome punishment included being split in two by a sword, with entrails spilling out.[7]

Growing up in Tulsa, Oklahoma, Dante's *Inferno* was required reading for eighth graders. I don't recall reacting negatively to Dante's portrayal of Muhammad's punishment when I first read it. When I ask others who have also read *The Inferno* whether they remember Muhammad's torment, few can. It is a simple, yet telling, example of how we Western Christians inherit attitudes toward Islam with little conscious thought or consideration.

Alongside the predominantly negative images of Islam that arose at the time of the Crusades, a handful of inquisitive and fair-minded church leaders sought to think differently about it. Francis of Assisi (1181–1226 CE) was, by far, the most visible Christian leader to challenge prevailing assumptions. In the midst of the Fifth Crusade (1217–1221 CE), Francis crossed battle lines in Egypt to meet with and preach to the Sultan. Francis's extraordinary initiative was consistent with his humility, commitment to nonviolence, and love of all creation. He, more than any other, provided the model for respectful dialogue and mutual witness that would take root among Western Christians in demonstrable ways beginning in the second half of the twentieth century.

Historians of the medieval period have highlighted a "moment of vision" and "a glimmering light of understanding" on the part of some Christians toward Islam in the fifteenth century.[8] The most vibrant manifestation of this positive spirit is found in the works of Nicholas of Cusa (1401–64). Nicholas immersed himself in political, ecclesiastical, and intellectual affairs through travel and reading. His *De pace fidei* (Concerning the harmony of the faiths) is an imaginary dialogue between members of different religious traditions. Set in a kind of heavenly council with seventeen participants, the dialogue presents a fundamental unity in religion though each community worships God using different names and ritual practices.

Nicholas's later work, *Cribratio alchorani* (Sifting of the Qur'an), attempts to distinguish the Christian and non-Christian elements in the Qur'an in order to refute the errors of Islam. Overall, Nicholas proffered a positive view of human religiosity as he constructively endeavored to engage issues of religious pluralism in general and Islam and the Qur'an in particular. Unfortunately, the "moment of vision" exemplified by Nicholas and others did not endure. The long-standing sentiment of animosity and deep hostility toward Islam prevailed. The dominant views were articulated clearly and forcefully in the far more influential works of a founding figure of the Protestant Reformation: Martin Luther (1483–1546 CE).

Luther's views about Islam were unambiguous. He lived and wrote in a time when the conquering armies of the (Muslim) Ottoman Turks were on the border of Austria. In his treatise *Von Krieg wider den Turken* (On War against the Turks), Luther calls the Turks' god "the devil" and the Turks "servants of the devil." Luther had access to portions of the Qur'an and expressed his desire to obtain a whole copy of the text so it could be translated into German. This, he argued, would enable everyone to see "what a vile and shameful book it is." Despite his limited access to the sacred text, Luther put forward his analysis of the Qur'an:

He (Muhammad) greatly praises Christ and Mary as being the only ones without sin, and yet he believes nothing more of Christ than that he is a holy prophet, like Jeremiah or Jonah, and denies that he is God's Son and true God. . . . On the other hand, Mohammed highly exalts and praises himself and boasts that he has talked with God and the angels. . . . From this anyone can easily see that Mohammed is a destroyer of our Lord Christ and his kingdom. . . . Father, Son, Holy Ghost, baptism, the sacrament, gospel, faith, and all Christian doctrine are gone, and instead of Christ only Mohammed and his doctrine of works and especially the sword is left.[9]

Luther and Dante not only reflect the consensus views among European Christians; their influence also far exceeded that of the rare alternative voices like Francis and Nicholas, who presented a far less confrontational approach to Muslims. Yet slowly, significant changes in ways of thinking and knowing began to emerge in the West in the seventeenth century, with the dawn of the Enlightenment.

From the Enlightenment to the Twentieth Century

The Enlightenment ushered in new ways of approaching what humans know and how to think about what is true, as traditional (often religious) sources of authority began to give way to scientific ways of evaluating and verifying data. Prior to the Enlightenment, stories of miraculous events were considered to be the definitive proof of a religion's veracity. But Enlightenment thinkers demonstrated that no miracle is ever self-authenticating, that depending on one's prior beliefs and presuppositions, different people will always interpret the nature and especially the meaning of "miraculous" events differently. As a result, many Enlightenment thinkers began to shift their focus away from miracle stories that defy normal experience to focus instead on moral and ethical wisdom within religions. This shift in perspective about what matters in religion made possible a new openness to Islam on the part of Western thinkers.

Thomas Jefferson is among the best-known figures to illustrate this new, rationalist worldview. Jefferson famously took a razor to the New Testament in order to cut out the parts about Jesus' performing miracles in order to focus on the life and morals of Jesus of Nazareth. Like many Enlightenment thinkers, Jefferson eschewed traditional stories and claims of supernatural events but remained convinced of the value of distilling the essence of Jesus' moral and ethical example and teachings.[10]

Jefferson also had a long-standing interest in Islam. He secured a copy of the Qur'an in 1765, eleven years before he wrote the Declaration of Independence. Jefferson continued to acquire and study books on Middle Eastern history and languages. His records include many notes reflecting on Islam in relation to English common law. Although he shared the prevailing disdain for Islam, he thought it important to study the religion. Drawing on Enlightenment ideas about toleration of religious differences, Jefferson was able to imagine Muslims as future citizens of the newly established United States. Vigorous debates about the role of religion in the new nation were often rancorous. Jefferson and others ultimately prevailed over those who argued for a Protestant nation as they laid the foundation for religious pluralism in a land where citizens could exercise freedom of religion and be protected from government-imposed religion.[11]

Distinct changes in Western Christian attitudes and patterns of relationships with Muslims in the past two centuries occurred in the context of the larger and more common interreligious encounter. Three significant developments contributed to new levels of understanding and intentional engagement: the rise of the academic study of religion; new means of transportation and communication facilitating international commerce and unprecedented levels of migration of people; and the modern global missionary movement led by European and American Christians.

Beginning in the nineteenth century, the self-consciously scientific study of religions marked a dramatic turning point in the pursuit of knowledge. In addition to scholarly pursuits in religious studies, pioneering work in various emerging disciplines—anthropology, history, philosophy, sociology, psychology, classical languages, and so on—contributed to a growing body of knowledge about the world's religious traditions. Insights and theories into ritual practices, doctrines, mystical traditions, and so forth provided data for comparative study of religion as a central feature of human life. The burgeoning academic study of religions stimulated scholars to amass a wealth of information on sacred texts, religious practices, and varying belief systems. Scholarship in the nineteenth century revealed how biased and simplistic were many of the monolithic views embraced uncritically by Western Christians over many centuries. Critical reflection and comparative studies effectively ushered in new ways of thinking about human religiosity.

These new approaches required careful scrutiny of deeply embedded biases. A simple example illustrates the point. Prior to the nineteenth century, Western scholars or church leaders whose biases did not influence their approach to the Qur'an were few and far between. Devout Muslims have routinely claimed "God says . . ." when quoting the Qur'an because they believe these are the very words of God revealed through the prophet Muhammad. On the other hand, earlier non-Muslim Westerners routinely quoted the Qur'an by saying, "Muhammad said . . ." This latter approach presupposes that these are not words directly from God but rather utterances of Muhammad. This is, of course, deeply offensive to Muslims, a direct rejection of a fundamental tenet of their faith. As more critical and scientific approaches to the study of religions began to take hold, it began to occur to Westerners that an unbiased approach was needed. Rather than assume that the Qur'an records God's words or that it preserves words originating with Muhammad, a nonjudgmental approach became available by simply reporting, "The Qur'an says . . ." That such a distinction was new is instructive.

The enhanced ability to travel and move more safely to all corners of the globe created an entirely new dynamic in the world. In addition to colonial powers dominating many distant lands, improved systems of transportation facilitated international commerce and made it possible for people to migrate to distant lands in search of a better life. Before the eighteenth or nineteenth centuries, many in the West may have known that there were Hindus, Buddhists, and Muslims in the world, but few would have interacted personally with such people. As more and more people from the Middle East, South Asia, and East Asia immigrated to Europe and North America, personal encounters with people of various religious traditions increased exponentially.

This ability to travel also inspired the great missionary movement of the nineteenth century. Christians in Europe and North America could now, for the first time, envision the realistic possibility of taking the gospel message to all people. Leaders of various Christian communions—Catholics, Baptists, Presbyterians, Lutherans, Methodists, Congregationalists, Disciples of Christ, and others—made plans and dispatched hundreds of missionaries in order to fulfill the Great Commission (Matthew 28:19–20).

In order to pursue the evangelistic missions and develop medical, educational, and other service ministries in distant lands, missionaries had to learn languages and study the cultures where they worked. While the primary motivations and orientation of many missionaries were not the same as Western scholars of world religions, there were often points of convergence in efforts to understand other religious traditions and practices. Actual human encounters with practitioners of other religions took the place of second-hand knowledge about those religions, deepening understanding. It is one thing to know that Muslims pray five times a day in the direction of Mecca and that they hope to make the Hajj at some point in their lives, to be physically present at the Ka'bah toward which they have oriented themselves multiple times each day. It is quite another thing to get to know Muslims and discover the personal and communal importance of daily prayers and experience firsthand the life-changing impact of fulfilling the lifelong dream of Hajj in the company of Muslims from many parts of the world.

Clearly, personal encounters made possible a post-Enlightenment shift in Western scholarship, from an impersonal examination of an "it" to an interpersonal dialogue with fellow human beings. Talking *about* people, their scriptures, and rituals is not the same as talking with them and observing how their faith and practices are manifest in their lives and communities. As more accurate knowledge of Islam, the Hindu traditions, and various Buddhist sects increased in the West, traditional Christian theological assumptions and long-standing exclusivist claims began to be reassessed more widely. While some scholars presented findings showing many points of commonality among outwardly differing religions, there were also many missionaries whose experiences raised serious questions concerning the polemical presuppositions about Christianity.

Two seminal events in the late nineteenth and early twentieth centuries demonstrate that era's ongoing opening to genuine interreligious understanding. The first was the World Parliament of Religions, held in Chicago in 1893, at which a number of non-Christian religious leaders made a powerful impact on the American public. The second was a series of three Christian world missionary conferences (Edinburgh, 1910; Jerusalem, 1928; and Tambaram, India, 1938). In retrospect, we can see from each of these conferences to the next an opening and widening theological appreciation of God's work within the other great religions of the world.

Debates among Christians on the meaning of religious pluralism and the best ways to pursue Christian mission, witness, and service continued after these great missionary conferences. However, two world wars, the end of colonialism, and the emerging new system of nation-states changed the landscape entirely in the first half of the twentieth century. The political reality of a postcolonial world stimulated a growing chorus of Christian leaders who shared the concerns about "spiritual imperialism" articulated earlier by some missionaries at the Jerusalem conference in 1928.

Major changes in approaches to Christian mission, service, and self-understanding were afoot in the aftermath of World War II. In 1948, the ecumenical movement was launched with the founding of the World Council of Churches (WCC) based in Geneva.

From the outset, the WCC and other ecumenical bodies began to explore interfaith issues. A four-day conference convened by the WCC's Departments of Evangelism and Missionary Studies in 1955 produced telling conclusions. The participants identified the need for in-depth study of the relationship between Christianity and non-Christian religions. They also insisted that far more was needed than simply to revive old debates. The conference proceedings prompted the creation of a special project to examine Christian faith in conversation with the world's other religions. In 1971 the WCC formally established two permanent subunits: one was commissioned to facilitate dialogue and cooperation between Christians and Jews; one was commissioned to facilitate dialogue and cooperation between Christians and people of other living faiths and ideologies.

Kenneth Cragg (1913–2012) was arguably the single most influential Western Christian leader to advance an accurate understanding of Islam and promote constructive Christian-Muslim relations during this formative period. Cragg, ordained in the Church of England in 1937, spent a great portion of his ministry as a bishop serving the Anglican dioceses in Lebanon, Palestine, and Egypt. Over the course of his life, he wrote eighteen books, primarily dealing with Islam, Christians, and Muslims in the Middle East, and also on Christian-Muslim relations. His first two books, *The Call of the Minaret* (1956) and *Sandals at the Mosque* (1959), were widely read and highly persuasive. Cragg modeled what many ecumenically oriented Christians were trying to balance, namely: a clear commitment to ministry as a faithful follower of Christ while also insisting on an accurate understanding of and appreciation for Muslims and Islam. Cragg and others provided the intellectual and theological foundation for the new institutional subunits established by the WCC in 1971.

There were also major developments under way among Roman Catholics, by far the largest group of Christians worldwide. New initiatives in interfaith relations were significant components within the broader framework of dramatic changes that emerged during the three years of the Second Vatican Council, or Vatican II. Between October 11, 1962, and December 8, 1965, leaders in the Roman Catholic Church addressed relationships between the Catholic Church and the modern world.

In the more than five decades since Vatican II, the Catholic Church has established secretariats guiding relationships between Catholics and non-Christian traditions, created and disseminated official church publications on interfaith issues, and organized interfaith dialogues at all levels—from international meetings to initiatives in local parishes. Chapter 5 explores various ways Christians and Muslims have pursued intentional initiatives in dialogue and cooperation in the past half century even as faithful adherents continue to pursue their respective mandates to bear witness to the truths they affirm God has revealed for the benefit of humankind.

First, however, we build upon this chapter's overview of conflict and cooperation. Understanding "how we got here" sets the stage for a clarifying examination of the world in which we are actually living today.

Questions for Discussion

1. This chapter challenges the widespread perception that Christians and Jews have always been in conflict with Muslims, and always will be. Where does that perception come from, do you think?

2. As Islam spread in the predominantly Christian lands, John of Damascus listed the ways it was similar to and different from Christianity. What would you put in each of those two lists?

3. The chapter explains that, while Christians have frequently said highly negative things about Muhammad, Muslims do not speak in a disparaging way about Jesus, Moses, and other biblical characters. What explains the difference?

4. Prior to reading this chapter, how conscious were you of images of Islam from Western literature such as Dante's *Inferno, The Canterbury Tales*, the writings of Martin Luther? Were you aware of the distinctive approach to

Muslims by Francis of Assisi or some of the positive contributions toward interfaith relations made by Christian missionaries?

5. Western Christian attitudes toward Islam started to change for some after missionaries and others began to spend more time with Muslim communities and individuals. What opportunities are there to do the same in your community?

Chapter Four

The World We Actually Live In

Islam in the Twenty-First Century

Being Muslim has become synonymous with pointed questions, with tension and mistrust, even with conflict. It has become a global phenomenon with profound consequences for inter-communal relations, political rhetoric and policies at the local, regional, national and international level.

Tariq Ramadan

Five weeks before the 2012 presidential election, Thomas Friedman, the celebrated columnist for the *New York Times*, published a particularly poignant Op-Ed article titled "The World We Actually Live In." Friedman's message was simple and straightforward: Candidate Mitt Romney's heated rhetoric and macho "solutions" to revolutionary upheavals and conflicts in the Middle East were dangerously simplistic and misleading. The campaign speeches and policy positions aimed at incumbent president Barack Obama were predictable fare for politicians. But, as Friedman clearly and cogently illustrated, the highly explosive conflicts were far more complex than charges of weakness or promises to deploy crushing military power could resolve. Friedman, a three-time Pulitzer Prize–winning author with expertise in the Middle East, foreign affairs, globalization, and the environment, pleaded for thoughtful, judicious, and nuanced use of power in the world we actually live in.[1]

69

Many countries were roiling in the fall of 2012 as the so-called Arab Spring or Arab Uprisings sparked popular revolutionary upheavals in Tunisia, Egypt, Libya, Yemen, Syria, and Bahrain. Friedman and other Middle East analysts endeavored to delineate common themes and distinct dynamics in various countries as they offered views on how the U.S. and other Western powers might respond most constructively to rapidly developing events. While Friedman's plea focused on a particularly volatile time and series of events, the same dynamics are readily visible in multiple times and settings. In confused and confusing times, many politicians, pundits, and religious leaders, with cocksure certainty, confidently advocate easy answers or simple solutions. Many seem oblivious to or unconcerned with the potential for counterproductive or unintended consequences that their calls to action might engender. In some instances, generic remedies for real or perceived problems include thinly veiled racism or bigotry aimed at groups deemed inferior, such as Muslims, African Americans, and Spanish-speaking immigrants seeking refuge at the southern border of the United States.

Our focus here is on Muslims and Islam. People of faith and goodwill must be willing to challenge easy stereotypes and deeply rooted biases about Islam and its 1.7 billion adherents. This requires some investment of time and energy to develop a more thoughtful, judicious, and nuanced understanding of the diversity and differences present among Muslims. The preceding two chapters have presented approaches to the necessary "unlearning" and learning required. We have employed three approaches: an explanation of the fundamental worldview most Muslims readily affirm, utilizing the foundational ritual-devotional duties manifest in the Five Pillars of Islam; a comparative reflection on how the Five Pillars are not at all alien to the beliefs and practices of Christianity and other major religions; and an overview of how conflicts and cooperation between Christians and Muslims over time have set the stage for our world today. We turn now to engage the most confusing issues, complexities, and recurring questions about Islam in the twenty-first century. What do non-Muslims need to know about Islam in the world we are actually living in?

Islam Is Not Monolithic: Can You Tell
a Sunni from a Shi'ite?

The tendency of many, if not most people, is to think of their own religion in terms of its ideal and other religions in terms of the flawed lived reality manifest by some of their adherents. Christians readily affirm that Jesus taught a gospel of love; Muslims are quick to declare that Islam is a religion of peace. While these fundamental truths are at the heart of the world's two largest religions, prominent examples of actions by self-declared believers contradict the ideal that these affirmations assert. Study the history of Christian anti-Semitism and the wry words of my friend Rabbi Balfour Brickner, now of blessed memory, ring painfully true: "Two thousand years of 'Christian love' is almost more than we Jews can bear!" How does one square "Islam as a religion of peace" with ready-to-die believers flying airplanes into buildings or exploding a bomb on a bus filled with innocent civilians or broadcasting the decapitation of a hapless Western journalist who had been taken hostage by religious zealots in Pakistan or Syria? Most Christians have some cognizance of the sordid history of the Crusades and Inquisitions, horrific religious wars between Christians in Europe, the Ku Klux Klan, and much more. And most Muslims are well aware that Islamic history includes many people and movements that have treated other Muslims and non-Muslims who disagreed with them in deplorable ways.

Knowing something of the fullness of one's own religious tradition makes it easier to continue to think generically of its ideal and assign repugnant behavior to the marginal extremes. Many people seem instinctively ready to place extremists completely outside the realm of "true Christianity" or "true Islam." But this explanation will not do. I've heard it many times—from Christians and Muslims—and I've challenged the flawed presuppositions that this stance employs. In the middle of the highly charged Iran hostage crisis, for instance, I encountered Muslims who were quick to distance themselves from the Ayatollah Khomeini by saying, "He's not a true Muslim." Yet I point out that millions of Muslims see him as their spiritual leader;

you can't simply remove large groups of people with whom you disagree from your broader religious community. Khomeini and his followers in their branch of Shi'ite Islam certainly think of themselves as devout Muslims. They are a minority among Muslims but nonetheless represent a substantial portion of what constitutes Islam today. There are many Christians with whom I disagree profoundly on all kinds of theological and moral issues—and plenty of people who don't agree with me theologically or otherwise at any given time—but I don't have the authority to dismiss others as though there is one clear form of "true Christianity." It is precisely this kind of purist thinking that fuels sectarian divisions and increasingly narrow forms of fundamentalism. On the other hand, the desire to acknowledge historic differences while bearing witness to the foundational unity that binds followers of Jesus together played a major role in the emergence of the Christian ecumenical movement in the twentieth century.

Islam, Christianity, and all other major religious traditions are extraordinarily diverse. None are monolithic. Be alert anytime you hear someone say (or find yourself saying), "Christians believe ___ [*fill in the blank*]." Stop and ask, "Which Christians? Do you mean Russian, Greek, Coptic, or Armenian Orthodox Christians? Are you referring to Quakers, Presbyterians, Baptists, Lutherans, or Methodists? Were you thinking of Roman, Maronite, or Syrian Catholics? Might you be speaking about Pentecostals in sub-Saharan African or snake-handling Pentecostals in the Appalachian Mountains? Or . . . ?" A quick search on the Internet reveals that there are somewhere between 33,000 and 41,000 identifiable Christian denominations in the world. These are roughly grouped into five main families of churches: Catholics, historic Protestants and Anglicans, Eastern and Oriental Orthodox churches, Pentecostals, and evangelical non-Pentecostals. There are more than fifty different types of Baptists in the U.S.! When someone says, "Christians believe . . . ," one can complete that statement with almost anything, and it is sure to apply to some group(s) of people who perceive themselves to be faithful followers of Jesus.

While Muslims have not splintered into as many factions as Christians through the centuries, the beliefs and practices within Islam are anything but monolithic. Various Muslim sects and communities have been and continue to be shaped by theology and history as well as by various cultural, national, and sometimes tribal contexts and traditions. When I teach undergraduate and graduate courses on Islam, I make it a high priority for the class to grasp this truth and begin to explore its multiple implications. I often assign *Islam Observed*, a short but highly informative book by Clifford Geertz, to illustrate the ways history and cultural context shape religious traditions. In this superb study, Geertz, longtime social anthropologist at Princeton University, utilizes "thick description" in his detailed analyses of Islam in Indonesia and Morocco. After spending years on the ground in these countries on the two ends of the predominantly Muslim lands, Geertz is able to paint a wonderful picture of Muslims who share affirmations about the Qur'an and the Five Pillars of Islam, yet live out their faith in strikingly different ways that connect with their historical and cultural context.[2]

Whereas Christian denominations can be roughly grouped into five "families," there are two main branches of Muslims: Sunnis and Shi'ites. Woven into the fabric of Islam in its many manifestations is a third broad category, the Sufis, those whose religiosity follows one of many mystical traditions. Sufis are not distinct from but present among Sunnis and Shi'ites. See the sidebar on pages 75–76 for an overview of early history that led to the Sunni-Shi'ite division. We will present additional information about Sufism shortly.

In the world in which we actually live, it is important—sometimes critically important—to understand the history and contemporary internal dynamics among Muslims. Jeff Stein posed the following question in an Op-Ed published by the *New York Times* in October of 2006: "Can You Tell a Sunni from a Shi'ite?" Three years into the U.S.-led war in Iraq, Stein's shocking article revealed how the large majority of top U.S. lawmakers and others making key decisions on policies had little to no idea who were Sunnis and who were Shi'ites or why it might matter.[3] This article came as virtual civil war between Sunnis and Shi'ites raged in Iraq while divisions between rival Shi'ite factions complicated the picture even more.

One cannot easily generalize about Sunni-Shi'ite relationships through the centuries for several reasons. Both of these larger groupings splintered in multiple ways, with four different and accepted schools of Islamic law among Sunnis, major sects and minor offshoot groups emerging among Shi'ites, a wide range of leaders in local/regional settings, and distinctive cultural and tribal traditions shaping beliefs and practices. One can easily identify all kinds of ways Sunnis and Shi'ites have lived together harmoniously. Traditionally, both Sunnis and Shi'ites participate together in the annual Hajj. Mixed marriages are not uncommon. At the same time, as with different Christian denominations, one can also find many examples of deep divisions and strong views on the errors of others' theology and practices.

Long-standing differences about rightful leadership are prominently or subtly woven into the fabric of Sunni-Shi'ite relationships, with Shi'ites most often in the position of being on the outside looking in. It is not surprising to see how themes of injustice in this world and redemptive suffering are vividly affirmed by Shi'ites in the annual events commemorating the martyrdom of Muhammad's grandson Husayn. But the historical reason for division is not the primary source of conflict in many lands today. Rather, when one explores the particular social, economic, and political dynamics in different lands, the contemporary roots of frustration and unrest become more evident. In Iraq and Lebanon, for instance, Shi'ites have comprised the majority community for many decades. But the political power—and with it most of the economic power—has been in the hands of Sunnis (Saddam Hussein and the Ba'athist Party in Iraq) and Christians (the Maronite Catholics in Lebanon), respectively. Without going deeper into close contextual analysis, one can recognize ways some of the internal conflict after the demise of Saddam Hussein related to Shi'ites, who had suffered tremendously under Saddam, becoming eager to "pay back" Sunnis, whom they perceived had benefited enormously at their expense. In Lebanon, the rise of Hizbollah

(Party of God) as a virtual state within a state was due in large part to the economic and political constrictions Shi'ites there had long endured while some Christians and Sunnis thrived.

Many Sunni-Shi'ite tensions are today lodged in the lands in the arc from Pakistan to Iran, Iraq, Syria, and Lebanon. Whereas Shi'ites comprise 10–13 percent of Muslims worldwide, they are 40–45 percent of the overall population in these countries.[4]

I've heard many people confidently assert that the fighting among Muslims in the Middle East is all about conflicts between Sunnis and Shi'ites. That is far too simplistic and misleading. Historic differences and long-held animosities are often woven into the convoluted mix, particularly in lands like those just noted that include large Shi'ite populations. But, as we've emphasized before, multiple issues combine in different lands and different conflicts in ways that require thoughtful contextual analysis to grasp. Knowing the differences and issues between and among Sunnis and Shi'ites in a given setting is often one of the key components in such contextual analysis.

Sunnis and Shi'ites

Timeline

- 632 CE: Death of Muhammad. Some support Ali, his first cousin and son-in-law, to lead the Muslim community as *Caliph*, but Abu-Bakr is chosen instead.
- 634–656: Ali passed over twice more before finally being chosen *Caliph*.
- 661: After five tumultuous years, Ali is assassinated. *Shi'at Ali* ("partisans of Ali"; origin of the term *Shi'a* or *Shi'ite*) insist that Ali's sons Hassan and Husayn, as grandsons of Muhammad, should lead. They, too, are passed over.
- 680: Civil war between the Shi'ites and the Sunnis (from *sunnah*, for those who follow the "practices" of Muhammad). Husayn decapitated, an event recalled annually on *ashura*, the most sacred day in the calendar for Shi'ites.

Beliefs and Practices

- The early Shi'ites continued to follow the guidance and teachings of the descendants of Muhammad; they called their leaders Imams.
- Shi'ites affirm that their Imams are guided by a divine inner light, meaning that the teachings of the Imams add to the authoritative guidance of the Qur'an and the Hadith. Sunni Muslims reject this possibility.
- Shi'ites came to venerate their Imams with shrines and pilgrimages and festivals, a practice that Sunnis also reject.
- Shi'ites believe that the last human Shi'ite Imam did not die but is being maintained by God and hidden in a special state of suspended animation (called *gayba*) until he will return to lead the faithful at the end of human history.

Branches and Divisions

- Sunnis account for more than 85 percent of the worldwide Muslim population, with the largest populations in Indonesia, Pakistan, India, and Bangladesh; various Shi'ites are intermingled throughout the world, with the highest concentration in Iraq, Iran, Bahrain, and Lebanon, where Shi'ites comprise the majority among Muslims in those countries.
- The Shi'ite Ismailis, the community headed by the Aga Khan today, believe the last Imam was the seventh.
- The Twelvers, the much larger group of Shi'ites, believe the twelfth Imam is the one whom God will bring back miraculously at the end of time.
- The Alawites, to which the Assad family (the rulers of Syria for almost half a century) belong, are a branch of Twelver Shi'ites.

A few words about Sufism also serve to deconstruct monolithic images of Islam. Very early on and throughout Islamic history, a sizeable portion of believers have pursued a less rigid, outwardly legalistic understanding of their religion. Known as Sufis, they use a time-honored tradition that verses in the Qur'an not only include outward meaning but also harbor deeper allegorical or metaphorical truths. In different ways Sufis have discovered and shared their treasured insights with others. Using poetry, metaphorical imagery, and ritual practices combining music with ecstatic dance, Sufis have sought to facilitate a continuing, intimate relationship with God. Many non-Muslims in the West will be aware of the brilliant poetry of Rumi and the Whirling Dervishes. These provide a popular glimpse into a much wider and deeper tradition of Islamic mysticism.

Many Sufis have run afoul of the more traditional practitioners by emphasizing the deeper meanings of unity with God over practices designed to remind believers daily of their Creator, Sustainer, and Judge. One famous example illustrates the point. After the call to prayer rang out over the city, Muslims who were making their way to the mosque noticed a man in his house playing with children. Thinking he may have not heard the call to prayer, a passerby called out to the man in the house that it was time for prayer. The response: "I am at prayer." The Muslims on the way to the mosque were not amused. For this Sufi, the five daily prayers were useful as long as one is in elementary school and needs the discipline of stopping what one is doing to remember God, the source of all creation. When one gets it and incorporates a constant remembering of God, such a person goes beyond the ritualistic disciplines and celebrates awareness of God in all things, including the joy of playing with children.

The larger point here is that scores of Muslims—Sunnis and Shi'ites—have embraced elements of Sufism throughout Islamic history and today. Because of a long history of distrust, misunderstanding, and persecution of numerous Sufis, many avoid drawing attention to their beliefs and practices. As I've gotten to know quite a few Muslims, I've discovered a significant number to have strong Sufi inclinations and inclusive theological perspectives not immediately obvious by their traditional outward practices. Islam is not monolithic.

Islam in the World of Nation-States

The emergence of the modern nation-state system is one of the most important and frequently overlooked factors shaping events and fueling conflicts today. For many centuries following the rise and spread of Islam in the seventh century, Muslims led the world with a brilliant civilizational system. Many fields of knowledge were developed or advanced by Muslims, including mathematics, philosophy, medicine, astronomy, navigation, horticulture, architecture, and chemistry. Islamic contributions to Western civilization are many and profound. When doctors in Europe were putting leeches on people to heal them, physicians in Baghdad had already figured out the circulatory system and were treating patients with delicate operations. Many English words beginning with "al" (the Arabic for "the") reflect their Arabic roots. Prominent examples include algebra, alchemy, alcohol. The number system we use—Arabic numerals—speaks to the Islamic contributions in mathematics.

Calling attention to the remarkable civilizational system with which Muslims led the world for many centuries provides a backdrop for what unfolded in more recent centuries. After the Mongol invasions in the middle of the thirteenth century and the later rise of the West, many lands comprising Islamdom began a long period of uneven decline and fragmentation. The global reach of European colonial powers—the British, French, Dutch, and Portuguese—systematically seized control of most Muslim-majority lands. Eventually even the Mughal Empire in India, the Safavid dynasty in Iran, and the Ottoman Empire in the Middle East gave way to Europe's imperial rulers. The first half of the twentieth century saw the end of colonialism and the emergence of the new world of nation-states. Most of the countries in the world today have come into being since the end of World War II. Understanding the impact and continuing legacies of colonialism is an essential though frequently and surprisingly overlooked ingredient in several contentious conflicts today.

Departing colonial powers not only drew sometimes artificial national boundary lines; they also frequently set up indigenous leaders who would continue to serve their interests, such as monarchs in Iraq and Egypt or the Maronite Christian control of Lebanon's government. In Egypt and Iraq the monarchs were soon overthrown in coups. Military strongmen grabbed power in Iraq, Syria, and Egypt. In Iran, the Shah was forced out in a popular election that brought Mohammad Mossadeq to power as Prime Minister. The significance of Mossadeq's democratic election was underscored when *Time* magazine named him Man of the Year in 1951. Mossadeq nationalized the oil companies and made clear that Iran would not continue to acquiesce to the interests of the British or the U.S. Then, in 1953, the newly installed administration of President Dwight Eisenhower orchestrated a coup that returned the Shah to power for the next twenty-five years.[5] The Iranian revolution ousting the Shah in 1979 was a harbinger of movements to replace indigenous, repressive rulers with more representative forms of government. Saddam Hussein was overthrown in the U.S.-led war in 2003, and elections followed; people in Tunisia, Egypt, Libya, Yemen, Syria, and Bahrain initiated revolutionary uprisings beginning in 2011 with the so-called Arab Spring.

Uniting in opposition to tyrannical rulers with horrific human rights records is understandable. Constructing new forms of participatory government in the world of nation-states is a monumental challenge. If you were to take a survey of representative, "average" citizens in the more than fifty-five Muslim-majority countries, I believe you would find that the large majority think that Islam can and should be a foundational component of whatever new government is to be fashioned. But if you asked those same people to sketch what they thought a twenty-first-century Islamic government structure would look like, you would find nothing close to consensus. Among Muslims, the awareness is widespread that Islam once led the world with a civilizational system that included religion and politics, plus economic, social, and military components. So too is the hope that Islam can once again be a basis for government in the new world of nation-states. No clarity or agreement on what this looks like means that we are likely to see a variety of experiments shaped by differing histories and circumstances in the coming two decades. While many serious and thoughtful Muslims in various settings advocate for and debate options for their country going forward, the challenges are compounded mightily by the presence of hard-line, violent extremists who claim to know what God wants for them and everyone else.

Islamophobia: A Cottage Industry

Previous chapters have identified and described ways in which several elements have all contributed to the fear of Islam so rampant in the West today: the rise and spread of Islamic civilization, widely held negative perceptions in Europe for centuries, and the more recent intense media coverage of destructive actions by extremists claiming inspiration from Islam. Given this broader framework, it is understandable that many non-Muslims are susceptible to facile explanations blaming Islam for revolutionary uprisings when many of the elements fueling unrest are similar to those present in mostly non-Muslim settings: brutally repressive governments whose power is not based on popular support; limited economic opportunities for the majority of people; and a history of social or ethnic discrimination or overt repression. This chapter seeks to widen the scope of knowledge about Islam in the world today. A more thoughtful and fair-minded understanding is made all the more difficult when so many people are visibly fanning the flames of Islamophobia.

In the first chapter we identified influential ways in which prominent political and religious leaders have used their public platforms to make highly charged and definitive pronouncements about the dangers posed by Islam and Muslims. Whether motivated by perceived political gain or theological convictions rooted in doctrinal purity or both, the negative images of Islam and Muslims permeate our society. The selected pronouncements or actions of these leaders serve as examples. The number of political and religious figures with national, regional, or local visibility can be expanded extensively to underscore how pervasive is the message that Islam and Muslims pose an existential threat.

In addition to politicians, preachers, and some self-appointed media pundits, a number of high-profile anti-Islam individuals and organizations have arisen in the years since the attacks on 9/11. Their mission—pursued through books, public speaking events, media interviews, and online resources—is clear: making certain non-Muslims know the "truth" about Islam, including the presumed goals of violent *jihad* against nonbelievers and the imposition of Sharia as part of the plan for world domination. These individuals and their organizations not only have become highly influential; their book sales and speaking engagements are also lucrative. They have effectively made Islamophobia a cottage industry in the U.S.

Frank Gaffney Jr. is a prime example. Gaffney, the founder and president of the Center for Security Policy, hosts a syndicated radio program (*Secure Freedom*), communicates with large audiences through social media, and is a ubiquitous presence on far-right radio and television programs. He was a guest more than forty times, for instance, on the *Breitbart News* program hosted by presidential advisor Steve Bannon. Gaffney has authored more than a dozen books or monographs, including *Shariah: The Threat to America*. His views are documented and summarized thoroughly by the Southern Poverty Law Center, a well-known organization dedicated both to fighting hate and bigotry and to seeking justice for the most vulnerable people in society. Gaffney is "gripped by paranoid fantasies about Muslims destroying the West from within."[6] In a manner reminiscent of Senator Joseph McCarthy, Gaffney ties all kinds of leaders to conspiracy theories about the Muslim Brotherhood or other Muslim groups that he labels as extremists, groups that he warns could soon destroy the U.S.

Lebanese American Brigette Gabriel is the founder of ACT for America, a group that claims to be America's largest national security grassroots organization. Gabriel, a Maronite (Catholic) Christian, was seriously injured as a child in 1975 when Muslim extremists destroyed her family home in Lebanon. While she acknowledges that most Muslims are peaceful, she claims that this is irrelevant because they do nothing to inhibit the 25–30 percent she believes are dedicated to the total destruction of the

West. The ACT for America website reports that Gabriel has appeared on more than 200 television and radio programs while the organization she heads reaches over one million people every day. Her 2018 book, *RISE: In Defense of Judeo-Christian Values and Freedom*, conveys her central messages and call to action before Islamic extremists prevail.

Many others, such as Robert Spencer and Pamela Geller, are well compensated for their speeches and book sales as they enjoy celebrity in a time when Islamophobia appears to be growing. Reinforcing deep-seated fears about "true Islam," and insidious activities they claim are being plotted or implemented by Muslims both here and around the world, seems to be a good way to make a handsome living these days. The purveyors of fear focus considerable energy on images of Jihad and Sharia. For many, these have become buzzwords guaranteed to evoke alarm. In truth, all practicing Muslims should be seeking to follow Sharia and engaging in Jihad. Demystifying the meaning of these central tenets of Islam can alleviate the sense of impending disaster being enhanced not only by fearmongers but also unwittingly by terminology commonly employed among many in the media.

The Meanings of Sharia and Jihad

Simply stated, Sharia is Islamic law based on the teachings of the Qur'an and the traditions of the Prophet. In its various manifestations, Sharia prescribes both religious and secular duties and sometimes penalties for civil or religious crimes. How and why did Sharia develop and become an essential component of Islam?

Chapter 2 explicated the foundational connotations contained in the first pillar of Islam, the Shahadah: "There is no god but God, and Muhammad is the messenger of God." God is the Creator, Sustainer, and ultimate Judge of creation. On the day of judgment, human beings will be accountable to their Creator. With eternity hanging in the balance, the most important questions become clear: What does God expect or require? On what bases will I be judged on that fateful day? As we noted, God has revealed what humans need to know through many prophets and messengers. Muslims affirm that God's revelation is preserved in the Qur'an. This sacred text provides the foundation for discerning God's will and requirements. The second source of authority is found in the example of the prophet Muhammad. Recall that the Qur'an identifies Muhammad as a "beautiful model" (Qur'an 33:21) and directs believers to refer matters to him (Qur'an 4:59).

The Qur'an addresses many issues but is silent on many others. And the Qur'an, like all sacred texts, still has to be interpreted. The Hadith (reports) on the sayings and actions (called the *Sunna*) add enormously to the guidance Muslims seek. Knowing what precisely the prophet said and did, however, presented a significant challenge.

From the outset, Muslims remembered and passed on whatever Muhammad said or did as the model to emulate. The Qur'an was collected and committed to writing within a decade of Muhammad's death. Reports about his sayings and actions, however, remained in oral tradition for many decades. Over time this became a serious problem. Since Muhammad's words supplementing the Qur'an effectively conveyed the force of law, people started to "remember" all kinds of things he said.

By the second century of Islam, scholars recognized that the presence of so many divergent Hadith required a thorough and reliable process to ascertain and preserve the authentic teachings and actions of the prophet. They developed a "science of Hadith," a sophisticated process whereby recognized scholars could assess the validity of a given Hadith based on the chain of transmission and the content of the saying or action. I took a semester course on Hadith during my doctoral studies. We carefully explored how some early Muslim scholars of the Qur'an and Hadith were able to reduce a massive body of sayings being attributed to Muhammad to a reliable corpus. Even with meticulous work to eliminate spurious sayings, the best scholars still found numerous examples where a definitive decision could not be achieved. The two widely accepted collections of Hadith contain many accounts with two or three slightly different versions of the occasion being referenced. A second indication of the scrupulous nature of this painstaking work is seen in the "grading" of Hadith. A saying that is certain to have been uttered by Muhammad will be graded "strong" and "reliable." Another version or a different Hadith might be graded to be "probable" or "weak," meaning that it cannot be discarded but there are problems preventing full affirmation of its authenticity.

The Qur'an and Hadith do not constitute a comprehensive system of law to guide individuals and the Islamic community (*ummah*). Two other sources were recognized as legitimate for developing Sharia: analogy and consensus. As with Western legal systems, Muslim jurisprudents having no clear guidance from the Qur'an or reliable Hadith can apply analogical reasoning, citing a legal principle established in another case. A final source of Islamic law is consensus. In the absence of authoritative sources, the collective wisdom or consensus of recognized jurisprudents is a valid source of law.

Sunni Muslims have long recognized four major schools of legal thought and practice, an explicit indication of valid variations in how Sharia is adjudicated. The most conservative form of Islamic law is found in the Hanbali tradition, the school of Sharia most notably utilized in Saudi Arabia, Afghanistan, and parts of Pakistan. The large majority of Sunnis follow less rigid approaches to Sharia. There are other variations among Shi'ites, who also look to the guidance provided by various Imams.

A second key point is this: Islamic law is always a work in progress. It is not stagnant since most Muslims affirm that changing times require changing rules. Initially, for example, the punishment for theft was to cut off the thief's hand. Soon it was recognized that different circumstances related to theft make a single punishment inappropriate and counterproductive. A destitute father who is caught stealing bread to feed five children, for instance, requires a more thoughtful punishment since removing his hand renders him even less able to care for five children.

A small percentage of Sharia deals with criminal codes; the majority of the provisions in the various manifestations of Sharia relate to personal conduct, traditions, and customs enshrined over time much like halakah is a comprehensive code of conduct for Jews guided by the Torah and Talmud. I know hundreds of practicing Muslims, and not one is interested in Sharia becoming the law of the land. They are committed to following the religious path as best they can know it.[7]

Confusion and fear about Sharia today is fueled in large part by the ways some Muslim extremists in groups like al-Qaida and ISIS and countries like Saudi Arabia, Afghanistan, and Pakistan have promoted a narrow and rigid framework for Sharia, including a return to the harshest forms of punishment—such as death by stoning for adultery and beheading for apostasy. It is important to recall that the vast majority of Muslims worldwide reject this extremist version of criminal punishment. When the Taliban ruled in Afghanistan during the 1990s, there were more than fifty-five countries in the world with Muslim majorities. But only three countries ever recognized the Taliban as the legitimate government in Afghanistan: Pakistan, Saudi Arabia, and the United Arab Emirates. Although most Muslims are appalled by horrific punishments like the capital punishments just noted or putting acid on the faces of women for not covering their faces appropriately in Afghanistan, the actions of extremists are a part of the contemporary struggle for the soul of Islam. Media coverage of gruesome and sensational acts perpetrated by Muslim extremists who claim to be implementing Sharia unfortunately feed the stereotypical images and Islamophobia in the West.

The term *jihad* is routinely used interchangeably with "holy war." Violent extremists are called (and sometimes call themselves) Jihadis. The term *jihad* simply means "struggling" or "striving." The two primary meanings of the term were made clear in a well-known Hadith. Upon returning from a battle against the Meccans, Muhammad famously told the Muslims they had just returned from the "lesser *jihad*" and must now engage the "greater *jihad*." The lesser jihad is the outward defense of Islam when the religion and Muslims are under attack. Muslims can and should defend the faith when under assault. The greater jihad, he explained, is the internal struggle each person has to know and do what is right. It is very much like the struggle in the flesh that the apostle Paul articulated in Romans 7:19: "For I do not do the good I want, but the evil I do not want is what I do."

The meanings of Jihad are lost in the popular understanding. The term has become synonymous with "holy war" in the West. The confusion has been enhanced by the various leaders—such as Saddam Hussein and Usama bin Laden—who declared Jihad on their perceived enemies but had no standing in Islam for issuing a call to "holy war." Most non-Muslims do not know that a formal call for "holy war" by qualified Muslim authorities has a long history and requirements fairly similar to the criteria necessary for declaring a "just war" that Christians developed over the centuries. Rather, the violent behavior of some Muslims who link their cause to Jihad reinforces the image of Islam as inherently violent and threatening. The violent responses of Muslim extremists to perceived insults directed toward Muhammad also add to the confusion and fear evoked for many by the buzzwords Sharia and Jihad.

Muslim Responses to Demeaning Depictions of Muhammad

Highly visible and violent reactions to demeaning portrayals of Muhammad in the West have understandably engendered much confusion and debate. While most Muslims are deeply offended by episodes described below, their theological perspective suggests that everyone is accountable to God. In the end, God will render justice. For some Muslims, however, degrading portrayals of Muhammad hit a deep nerve so painfully that they demand a strong response. Consider the following examples.

In 1988, an international storm erupted immediately after the publication of Salman Rushdie's book *The Satanic Verses*. Rushdie, an atheist born into a Muslim family in northern India, explicitly incorporated several of the long-standing derogatory images of Muhammad and Islam into his novel. Rushdie and many literary critics claimed that the novel was not fundamentally about Islam but rather about alienation, the experience of being caught between two cultures, and the dangers of absolutist belief systems. Many Muslims sharply disagreed, decrying the book as blasphemy and an overt mocking of their faith. In India the book was banned as hate speech directed toward Muslims. In February of 1989, Iran's Ayatollah Khomeini issued a *fatwa* (an authoritative legal opinion) calling for Rushdie's death. Attempts to kill Rushdie were thwarted, and he required police protection for years as the furor continued.

On November 2, 2004, Dutch television and film actor and director Theo van Gogh was assassinated on the streets of Amsterdam. The assailant was a Dutch Moroccan Muslim man who was infuriated by van Gogh's 2004 film, *Submission*. The film, which van Gogh prepared in close consultation with the Somali-born Dutch politician and author Ayaan Hirsi Ali, is sharply critical of ways women are treated in many predominantly Islamic lands.

Another controversy attracting international attention arose in 2005, when the Danish newspaper *Jyllands-Posten* published twelve cartoons depicting Muhammad. The newspaper defended their publication as an effort to contribute to debates about criticism of Islam and issues of media self-censorship. Muslims in Denmark and around the world reacted strongly for two reasons: as an aniconic tradition, most Muslims have always avoided any visual depiction of the prophet; and in various ways the cartoons published were intentionally demeaning. For several months, protests and riots broke out in many Muslim-majority lands, where Danish and other embassies as well as several Christian churches were attacked. Some two hundred people died in the violent clashes arising in the months after the publication of the cartoons. The controversy also sparked heated debates and reproductions of the cartoons among various Western media. For some, the overriding issues centered on freedom of expression and/or where to draw the line (if any line is to be drawn) with self-censorship in deference to religious sensitivities.

Other violent responses to visual depictions of Muhammad were twice directed at the offices of *Charlie Hebdo*, a French satirical publication. Terrorists bombed the Paris offices of *Charlie Hebdo* in 2011 after its publication of political cartoons making fun of Muhammad. On January 7, 2015, armed men burst into those same offices and opened fire on writers and staff, killing twelve people before fleeing as they declared, "The prophet has been avenged."

Such attacks must be flatly condemned. Even if those publishing offensive cartoons are deliberately demeaning in their satirizing Islam or Muhammad, such atrocious violence is never justified. In my experience, however, deeply disturbing developments like those just noted can provide opportunities for serious and potentially constructive interfaith dialogue, a central focus of the next chapter. Before we turn to that chapter, some attention to Islam in contemporary America is in order. This will not only serve to further deconstruct monolithic images of Islam but also provide helpful information to facilitate interfaith dialogue in the world we actually live in.

Islam in America

In my class World Religions in America, students are often surprised to discover the great diversity of religious traditions all around them. This religious pluralism did not develop overnight, of course. People from various backgrounds reflect distinctive histories and experiences. For our study, it is particularly important to reflect broadly on the stories shaping the Muslim communities in twenty-first-century America. As we have noted, many Americans harbor deep-seated fears about radicalized citizens after 9/11 and the supposed Muslim goal of global domination or the destruction of Western civilization propagated by some politicians, preachers, and leading Islamophobes.

Several different streams contribute to the composition of diverse Muslim communities in America today. We find names of African Muslims among the ranks of people fighting against the British in the Revolutionary War. A significant percentage (perhaps 15–25 percent) of Africans who were captured and forcibly brought to America as slaves were Muslims. The highly acclaimed 1977 television series *Roots* and the 1997 movie *Amistad* highlight this religious component of the slave trade in America. The large majority of Muslims in America, however, are connected to families who immigrated from various parts of the world during the great influx in the late nineteenth and early twentieth centuries and again after the 1965 Immigration and Naturalization Act was passed by Congress. As people get to know their Muslim neighbors, they will find many third-, second-, and first-generation Americans as well as some who have only recently become citizens.

African American Muslims comprise another major component of Islam in America. The Nation of Islam or Black Muslim movement arose to prominence as an indigenous American group under the leadership of Elijah Muhammad. He led the group from 1934 until his death in 1975 and was a mentor to Malcolm X, Louis Farrakhan, and heavyweight boxer Muhammad Ali. The highly controversial group began to shift away from unorthodox and hostile views against Jews and Caucasians in the early 1960s as Malcolm X became convinced in the truth of inclusive, mainstream Sunni Islam. In 1976, Elijah Muhammad's son and successor, Wallace D. Muhammad, formally adopted traditional Sunni Islam and changed the name from the Nation of Islam to the American Society of Muslims. A segment of the former group, perhaps 15–20 percent, remained under the leadership of Louis Farrakhan, but the large majority of African American Muslims today see themselves as one with the larger Muslim community.

Intermarriage and conversion are other paths through which some Americans have become Muslims. I have known a number of Muslim couples where one spouse converted before marriage or when they got married. The same is true for a number of Jewish and Christian friends, too. Some Americans have come to Islam on their own as converts persuaded by the message and truths they discovered or being drawn in through the mystical paths illuminated by Sufism. Again, as people become acquainted with more and more American Muslims, they will discover the various ways people have been born into or found their way into Islam.[8]

I close this chapter with information about Islam in Oklahoma, the state I actually live in. Muslims comprise less than 1 percent of the population in Oklahoma, well below the estimated 3–4 percent of the U.S. population. A substantial majority of American Muslims are highly educated, including a disproportionate number of medical doctors both nationally and in Oklahoma. In each of my state's two largest cities, Oklahoma City and Tulsa, there are currently between 450 and 500 Muslim practicing physicians: cardiologists, oncologists, urologists, anesthesiologists, and so on. These numbers are five to ten times higher than the percentage of Muslims in the state might suggest. Two brothers from Iran own the largest home building company in Oklahoma. They came in the 1970s to study architecture at the University of Oklahoma but had difficulty getting jobs after graduation. From humble beginnings they started their own business and built it into an American success story. They became U.S. citizens with children and grandchildren born here. They are well known throughout the state and region for their generous support of higher education and numerous charitable organizations helping people in need domestically and around the world.

There are many Muslims in higher education. When Oklahoma State University President Burns Hargis hosted the first Iftar (a dinner celebrating the breaking of the fast during Ramadan), he was surprised to learn that there were forty-two Muslims serving on the full-time faculty at the university. The Imam from Oklahoma City and I were speakers at the event where over three hundred people—faculty, staff, and families—came in response to the invitation of the university's president. Similar numbers of Muslims are tenured or tenure-track faculty teaching engineering, business, modern languages, history, philosophy, and other courses at the University of Oklahoma as well.

These statistics and examples stand in stark contrast to the fears and perceptions of many Oklahomans. In 2010, Oklahoma citizens passed a referendum banning Sharia from the state. The referendum, which was the first of its kind in the U.S., passed with a 70 percent plurality. Although a federal court subsequently ruled the measure unconstitutional, the overwhelming support validated the influence of those claiming that Muslims were somehow working to destroy the West and replace our legal system with Islamic law. I've discussed this referendum with more than a hundred clergy in the state over several years and found most to be fearful of Sharia; yet only three could actually describe what Sharia is or how it is supposed to guide faithful Muslims in their daily life.

These brief examples illustrate both the depth of fear and misinformation but also point to the hopeful resources available to people of faith and goodwill who wish to move forward constructively in the world we actually live in.

Questions for Discussion

1. Why is it important to understand that Islam is not monolithic?
2. How would you begin to describe Sharia to a friend or relative who had expressed their conviction about the danger(s) it posed? What questions would you like to ask Muslims about Sharia?
3. Having read the chapter, how would describe the main differences between Sunnis and Shi'ites?
4. Why do individuals and organizations find it profitable to feed fears about Islam? What benefit do they derive?
5. When Western media publish cartoons or demeaning descriptions of Muhammad, some Muslims express deep anger and resentment—in some cases, even violence. How should we balance the values of free expression with respect for the beliefs of others?

Chapter Five

Faithful Response to Two Imperatives

The Missionary Mandate and Interfaith Dialogue

> Now the eleven disciples went to Galilee, to the mountain
> to which Jesus had directed them. When they saw him,
> they worshiped him; but some doubted. And Jesus came
> and said to them, "All authority in heaven and on earth has
> been given to me. Go therefore and make disciples of all
> nations, baptizing them in the name of the Father and of
> the Son and of the Holy Spirit, and teaching them to obey
> everything that I have commanded you. And remember, I
> am with you always, to the end of the age."
>
> Matthew 28:16–20

The Gospel of Matthew concludes with Jesus' final words to
his disciples known as the Great Commission. The earliest
written documents in the New Testament are letters from the
apostle Paul, the missionary to the Gentiles. Together with the
Acts of the Apostles, Paul's letters to communities in Asia Minor,
Greece, and Rome record some of the ways the earliest followers
of Jesus sought to spread their message of Jesus' life, death, and
resurrection; baptize new believers; and deal with various challenges arising in the growing churches. From the beginning, followers of Jesus have pursued the missionary mandate at the heart
of the religion.

At the same time, Christians understood that Jesus taught a
gospel of love through which he set forth God's expectations for

those who would faithfully follow him. Jesus called his disciples to be peacemakers, to resist returning evil for evil, to turn the other cheek and even pray for those who persecute them, to respond compassionately when they encounter people in need of food, water, clothing, or support when sick or in prison. The foundational requirements are communicated clearly through a well-known encounter recorded in the Gospel of Luke. When asked by a lawyer what he must do to inherit eternal life, Jesus turns the question back on the man and asks, "What is written in the law? What do you read there?" The man responds, "You shall love the Lord your God with all your heart, and with all your soul, and with all your strength, and with all your mind; and your neighbor as yourself." Jesus confirms this as the correct answer and says simply, "Do this, and you will live." But the man responds with another question, "And who is my neighbor?" Jesus replies with the parable of the Good Samaritan (Luke 10:25–37).

Paul, who modeled the missionary imperative most visibly in the New Testament, also proffered a great deal of guidance to the communities of faith he helped establish. He reinforces Jesus' teachings as conveyed in the canonical Gospels. Recall Paul's letter to the Christians gathered in Rome where he describes succinctly the marks of a true Christian:

> Live in harmony with one another; do not be haughty, but associate with the lowly; do not claim to be wiser than you are. Do not repay anyone evil for evil, but take thought for what is noble in the sight of all. If it is possible, so far as it depends on you, live peaceably with all. (Romans 12:16–18)

The followers of Jesus have a clear missionary mandate and a responsibility to be engaged in a ministry of compassion for those in need, peacemaking, and reconciliation in a broken and hurting world.

Islam is also a missionary religion. Muslim self-understanding begins with the conviction that God has revealed what human beings need to know and do one last time through the prophet Muhammad. The day of judgment is coming, but God's revelation and necessary guidance is now available to all in the Qur'an and the example of the prophet. The Arabic term for inviting people to the faith is *da'wah*. The Qur'an instructs believers to do as Muhammad and other prophets have done:

> Call [or invite] to the way of your Lord with wisdom and goodly exhortation. And dispute with them in the most honorable manner. Surely your Lord is He Who knows best those who stray from His way, and He knows best the rightly guided. (Qur'an 16:125, auth. trans.)

Muslims are enjoined to invite others to the way of God in sincerity, with reason, and without coarseness. In a parallel passage, the faithful are reminded to "dispute not with the People of the Book [Jews and Christians], except in the most kindly manner" (Qur'an 29:46, auth. trans.). God has taken the initiative as a mercy to humankind. Recall that 113 of 114 chapters in the Qur'an begin with the affirmation that God is the most Merciful and the most Compassionate. The goal of *da'wah* is to invite others to a better understanding of how to worship God directly and through one's actions. Traditionally, the conversation directed at non-Muslims centers on the meaning of the Qur'an and how Islam works for believers. It is up to people individually how they will respond to this invitation. Faith cannot be coerced but must be embraced freely and intentionally. The Qur'an states this succinctly in a frequently cited verse: "There can be no compulsion in religion" (Qur'an 2:256).

Islam, like Christianity, directs the faithful to love and worship God while also loving and showing compassion for humans. The Qur'an contains many clear directives about human responsibilities toward the poor, the widow, the orphan, the elderly, and so forth. Two of the Five Pillars of Islam discussed in chapter 2, the fast during Ramadan and the obligation of charitable giving, underscore the requirement to help those in need. Various passages in the Qur'an that deal with the day of judgment parallel the focus of Jesus' teachings on the criteria for heavenly reward or punishment, as in the Judgment of the Nations in Matthew 25 and the parable of the Rich Man and Lazarus in Luke 16, both cited in chapter 2 above.

Christianity and Islam are two of the three major world religions that are missionary in orientation; Buddhism is the third such religion.[1] Other religions that have stood the test of time have had some periods where certain groups were committed to missionary activity, but the primary way most religions have sustained and perpetuated their traditions is through procreation. Given the centrality of the missionary obligation, it is not surprising that Christianity and Islam are the two largest, most widespread, and fastest-growing religious traditions in the world today. As we have seen, the deeply ingrained missionary impulse should be framed by a manifestation of God's love for all of creation and the peace that comes with knowing and doing God's will. Unfortunately, zealous adherents in both religions have often failed to live up to these ideals.

Many examples of intolerance, pressured adherence, or forced conversion are present in the history of both religious traditions. A quick survey of church history reveals a dismal record of hostility and persecution directed toward Jews, Muslims, and other Christians who were deemed to be heretical for whatever reasons. The history of anti-Semitism, Crusades, Inquisitions, brutal religious wars in Europe, and missionary-related abuses in the Americas—all underscore the point. While there is little evidence of Islam spreading by forced conversion at the point of a sword, rapid military conquests plus economic and social pressures were often compelling to those who might otherwise feel like second-class citizens. In many settings—including many predominantly Muslim lands today—severe penalties, including death, have been meted out to Muslims who leave the faith and openly embrace Christianity. In many predominantly Muslim countries, it is illegal for Christians to proselytize.[2] Blasphemy laws prohibiting insults or irreverence toward God or the Prophet remain in place in many countries with differing levels of enforcement. We have noted how demeaning depictions of Muhammad strike a nerve and often provoke violent responses in ways that defy the cardinal tenet in the Qur'an that there can be no compulsion in religion.

The point here is that the actions of zealous, mission-oriented Christians and Muslims have often fallen far short of the ideal espoused by most adherents in both traditions. At the same time, missionaries and people of goodwill sharing their faith have made life-changing contributions as they have carried their messages and lived out their faith constructively around the world. The example of Indonesia springs to mind. Indonesia is the largest Islamic country in the world, with over 230 million Muslims. Islam did not arrive or spread through these islands by military force. Rather, Islam flourished by the power of its message and the living examples of commercial traders and merchants who traveled and settled there. Western Christian missionaries also made many life-changing contributions as they ventured into distant corners of the world in the nineteenth century. Their work often brought substantial improvements in health care, education, and economic opportunity, along with their witness about God's saving grace through the life, death, and resurrection of Jesus.

Christian Mission and the Ecumenical Movement

Chapter 3 introduced elements of the changing landscape facilitated by improved means of transportation. Looking back, we can see several ways the nineteenth- and twentieth-century missionary movement anticipated and nurtured the ecumenical movement, stimulated theological reflection on questions of Christian faith in a religiously plural world, and laid the foundation for the dramatic new initiatives for interfaith dialogue in the second half of the twentieth century.

When developing plans for the great missionary expansion in the nineteenth century, leaders of many Western Christian denominations realized that they could not effectively support missionaries all over the world. So, despite the theological differences that had divided them in the past, the Presbyterians, Methodists, American Baptists, Congregationalists, and others entered into comity agreements. They effectively divided up the world in order to facilitate widespread mission initiatives and avoid direct competition with one another.

The longer-term impact of this division of labor was still very visible in the Middle East in the 1980s, when I coordinated the mission and service ministries of forty-two denominations as the Director of the Middle East Office at the National Council of Churches of Christ in the USA (NCCCUSA), based in New York. In the comity arrangements, the Presbyterians were responsible for Syria, Lebanon, Egypt, and Iran. Today, Presbyterians (who are called Evangelicals there) comprise the dominant form of Protestant Christianity in those lands. They are organized in the Synod of the Nile and the Synod of Syria and Lebanon.[3] The old Congregational churches of New England (now part of the United Church of Christ) focused their mission in Turkey. The Methodists concentrated in North Africa, primarily Algeria, Tunisia, and Morocco. The Reformed Church in America went to Oman and the Gulf States. These comity arrangements anticipated the formal, organized rise of the ecumenical movement. Leaders in various churches had come to understand that a greater good was served more by cooperating than by competing with one another for adherents. They were saying, in effect, how that which binds Christians—at least most Protestants—together was far more important than the things that had caused division in the past.

Building on this same affirmation of unity in what the apostle Paul calls "the body of Christ," many of the missionaries encountered long-standing Christian communities in place. Most of the Christian communities with whom I worked in the Middle East were part of the Oriental Orthodox family of churches: Coptic Orthodox, Syrian Orthodox, and Armenian Orthodox. These churches had been largely ignored in Europe and the West after they were declared heretical in 451 CE at the Council of Chalcedon. They were derisively labeled "monophysite" because they were perceived as placing too much emphasis on the divinity of Jesus when the accepted doctrine declared Jesus to be 100 percent divine and 100 percent human. Rather than dissolve when rejected by what would come to be the Roman Catholic and Eastern Orthodox Churches, the bishops of these ancient communions returned to their homelands and continued to live and worship. These churches have functioned independently, operating monasteries and selecting their own bishops, patriarchs, and, in the case of the Copts, popes.

There are also Eastern Orthodox Churches (known in the West as Greek, Serbian, and Russian Orthodox), most notably the Antiochian Orthodox Church, as well as various Catholic communions: Maronites in Lebanon, Roman Catholics, Greek Catholics or Melkites, Coptic, Syrian, and Armenian Catholics. Even less well known is the Assyrian Church of the East (largely in Iraq).[4] The presence of these Christian communities who had lived alongside Muslims for over a thousand years raised important and challenging issues for the Western missionaries. As one might expect, the relationships developed between missionaries and Christians in regions like the Arabic-speaking Middle East didn't follow a single pattern. Some deemed indigenous Christians theologically deficient; others sought ways to collaborate over time. In some settings, Western Christians, frustrated by the small numbers of Muslims converting to the Christian faith, turned their attention to local Christians and engaged in what euphemistically has been called "sheep stealing."

The U.S.-based Presbyterians were the most widespread in the Arabic-speaking Middle East. In addition to establishing congregations and training local pastors in Egypt, Syria, Lebanon, and Iran, they also engaged in social service ministries by building and staffing clinics, hospitals, schools, and agricultural and other sustainable ventures to enable longer-term economic stability for indigenous Christians and non-Christians alike.

Many missionaries and some scholars who were practicing Christians sought more substantial engagement with people of other faiths. Learning languages, translating and studying sacred texts, entering into dialogue, observing or participating in rituals or celebrations—all these stimulated both the comparative study of religion and theological reflection on Christian particularity in the midst of religious pluralism. The records and subsequent accounts as well as books produced by the aforementioned world missionary conferences in Edinburgh (1910), Jerusalem (1928), and Tambaram (1938) reflect the insights and animated debates among missionaries and denominational leaders during this time before and after World War I.

The collective experiences in the century after Western Christians launched the great missionary movement in the early 1800s laid the foundation for the profound changes that began to take institutional form in the middle of the twentieth century. The World Council of Churches (WCC) was formed in 1948. This global Christian ecumenical organization initially included 147 communions who were committed to working together to bear witness to Christian unity and maximize effective stewardship of resources for service ministries. Two years later, NCCCUSA was founded in New York City. Other regional, state, and local councils or conferences of churches appeared in subsequent decades as the ecumenical movement spread around the world.

The Middle East Council of Churches (MECC) was established in a historic assembly uniting Orthodox and Protestant churches in 1974. For the first time since the Council of Chalcedon in 451 CE, Oriental and Eastern Orthodox Christian bishops, patriarchs, the Coptic Orthodox pope, and the Armenian Orthodox Catholicos sat together in mutual affirmation. In 1990, with the full blessing of Rome, the Catholic churches in the Middle East accepted the invitation to join with the two families of Orthodox churches and Protestants in making the MECC the first ecumenical body to include all branches of Christianity under one umbrella organization. I was serving as the Middle East Director for the NCCCUSA and was privileged to be at the historic assembly where the MECC General Secretary opened the convocation with these words: "This is the place where the Christian church began. This is where the Christian church began to splinter and divide. It is most appropriate that this is now the first region where all branches of Christianity join together to bear witness to the unity in the body of Christ."

The ecumenical movement gave visible symbolism to Christian unity. But it also had far-reaching consequences in shaping the future of Christian mission and service. Henceforth, ecumenically committed communions in Europe and the U.S. resolved to be in "mutual mission" with the Christians in the Middle East and other regions. Put another way, those churches that had sent missionaries beginning in the nineteenth century were now affirming that the indigenous Christians in the Middle East were the body of Christ there. Future mission and service ministries would be coordinated with and normally supervised locally by Middle Eastern Christians. Two examples from my experience facilitating ecumenical work with Middle Eastern Christians on behalf of the forty-two member churches of the NCCCUSA illustrate this new orientation.

In 1975 Lebanon was plunged into a fifteen-year, multisided, and convoluted civil war. Christians in the U.S. understandably wanted to help injured and displaced people in a country where the needs for food, shelter, clothing, medical care, and so on were staggering. The pragmatic wisdom of ecumenism proved invaluable. Rather than having forty-two different communions trying to communicate, secure what was most needed, and coordinate procurement and shipping of materials, all of those responsibilities converged on my desk. I and my staff communicated with the MECC staff on all the logistics while we organized financial, material, and human resources from Methodists, Presbyterians, Episcopalians, Lutherans, Quakers, and many others. Not only was this efficient in getting needed supplies and personnel to the MECC for their service ministries; it was also responsible stewardship of resources. By minimizing bureaucratic costs in both the U.S. and Lebanon, over 90 percent of the financial resources from U.S. churches and Church World Service, the ecumenical relief and development arm of the NCCCUSA, reached the people in need.

At different times during the 1980s, the newly formed Evangelical Lutheran Church in America (ELCA) and the United Methodist Church mission boards wanted to support a missionary in Jerusalem. As we worked on plans ecumenically, both denominations agreed to provide full support for a missionary or missionary family that would be given to the MECC for whatever ministry assignments were most needed. Rather than try to start First Methodist Church in Jerusalem, the United Methodists Board of Global Missions instead provided human and financial support for the work of Middle Eastern Christians.

Ecumenical relationships enabled Western and Middle Eastern Christians to learn from one another in various ways. One of the most powerful lessons centered on the definitions of mission and service in lands where it is illegal to proselytize. Christians in the Middle East emphasized presence, witness, and service. They helped Western evangelicals understand that Christians are not responsible for converting anyone. It is God who works in the hearts of people. Followers of Jesus are responsible to bear witness to the good news in their lives and ministries to others. Providing medical care plus educational and economic opportunities for all people in their settings is a powerful form of witness, the results of which may or may not be visible in terms of church membership or growth.[5]

Finally, the social service ministries by local Christians in the Middle East had benefits going beyond the help they provided for Christians and non-Christians alike. They represented a positive message of reconciliation, interdependence, and hope. Such direct, personal encounters also fostered interfaith dialogue and friendships.

Interfaith Dialogue Established by the WCC and the Vatican

The world's two largest institutional representatives of global Christianity—the WCC and the Vatican—instituted intentional programs for Christian dialogue with Muslims, Jews, Hindus, and Buddhists as well as multifaith dialogue events beginning in the 1960s. In my experience, a substantial portion of Catholics, Protestants, and Orthodox Christians continue to be either unaware or poorly informed about these initiatives. A brief overview will help clarify the orientation and decisions by leaders in all branches of Christianity to incorporate efforts that foster interfaith understanding and cooperation as a vital component of the work of their churches. Put another way, the urgent need for interfaith understanding and cooperation today was already understood as a priority for Roman Catholics and most Protestant and Orthodox Christian leaders more than half a century ago.

Throughout the decade of the 1960s, leaders in the WCC organized dialogue meetings and internal discussions to determine how best to pursue what they perceived as the dialogical imperative. This bold initiative grew out of the awareness of a long history of religious conflict and the insights gained from the Christian missionary endeavors and debates discussed above. Interfaith dialogue was understood as a logical extension of the mutual respect and desire for constructive cooperation manifest in the ecumenical movement.

After a decade of deliberations and consultations, the WCC established the subunit for Dialogue with People of Living Faiths and Ideologies (DFI). They launched a multifaceted series of programs over the next two decades with three major foci. The DFI organized large international and smaller regional dialogue meetings, produced and distributed educational materials to help churches improve understanding of other religions, and worked with other subunits to facilitate reflection on Christian mission and theological issues connected to religious pluralism. The international initiatives focused on Christian-Muslim dialogue centered on major gatherings in Broumana, Lebanon, in 1972, and Columbo, Sri Lanka, in 1982. The first international meeting included 46 participants (25 Christians and 21 Muslims) from 20 countries for a week of deliberations. The Columbo meeting was even larger, with 33 Muslims coming from 22 countries and 30 Christians from 27 countries. With these major gatherings and discussions in the interim, there were strong affirmations of the necessity for improving mutual understanding and fostering cooperation, especially at the local level. At the same time, participants were wary of any effort to suppress differences or be satisfied with the lowest common denominator. Rather, they determined to explore points of convergence and disagreement frankly and self-critically. This chapter concludes with more on the types of dialogue, insights, and accomplishments from these and other multireligious meetings organized by the WCC and the Vatican.

For Roman Catholics, by far the largest group of Christians in the world, organized interfaith dialogue was a direct result of the Second Ecumenical Council of the Vatican (October 11, 1962, to

December 8, 1965), known also as Vatican II. Vatican II can be described as the Roman Catholic Church's contemporary effort to understand itself and its ministries in light of the challenges of modernity in the era after World War II. The process of introspection lasted years and included over 2,500 participants at times. While many people will recall changes such as dropping the requirement of Mass being conducted in Latin in favor of vernacular languages, the Council produced sixteen official documents on a wide range of subjects. Three of the official documents deal explicitly with interfaith relations.[6] The document titled "The Declaration on the Relations of the Church to Non-Christian Religions" (*Nostra Aetate*) provided the most direct and detailed guidance for the future. Promulgated on October 28, 1965, by Pope Paul VI, *Nostra Aetate* is divided in five sections. The first section speaks of the oneness of the human family and affirms "God's providence, evident goodness and saving designs" for all people. The second section acknowledges the values found in other religions and declares that the Catholic Church "rejects nothing of what is true and holy in these religions" and puts forth a call for dialogue:

> The Church, therefore, urges her sons [*sic*] to enter with prudence and charity into discussion and collaboration with members of other religions. Let Christians, while witnessing to their own faith and way of life, acknowledge, preserve and encourage the spiritual and moral truths found among non-Christians, also their social life and culture.[7]

The third section concentrates specifically on Christian-Muslim relations. It provides a new orientation toward faithful adherents of Islam:

> The Church has also a high regard for Muslims. They worship God, who is one, living and subsistent, merciful and almighty. . . . They strive to submit themselves without reserve to the hidden decrees of God, just as Abraham submitted himself to God's plan, . . . and they await the day of judgment and the reward of God following the resurrection

from the dead. For this reason, they highly esteem an upright life and worship God, especially by way of prayer, alms-deeds and fasting.[8]

The document pleads with both Christians and Muslims to forget the many quarrels and dissentions of the past centuries in order to make a sincere effort to achieve mutual understanding and work jointly to preserve and promote peace, liberty, social justice, and moral values.

Institutional support for these emerging initiatives took the form of a new Secretariat for Non-Christian Religions. This Secretariat was charged with two primary tasks: (1) studying the different religious traditions and providing resources for both Christians and non-Christians; and (2) promoting interreligious dialogue through education and by facilitating efforts by bishops and others at the local level.[9] Over two decades later, the Secretariat was renamed the Pontifical Council on Interreligious Dialogue. We will return to the formation of the dialogue subunits at the WCC and the types of dialogue programs pursued by the Vatican Secretariat and WCC shortly. First, it is particularly instructive to highlight ways Pope John Paul II (pontiff in 1978–2005), the most visible Christian leader for over a quarter century, lived out the interfaith vision and mandates of Vatican II.

In 1985, for instance, Pope John Paul II addressed 80,000 Muslims at a football stadium in Casablanca. Consider the timeliness of his words more than three decades later:

> We believe in the same God, the one God, the Living God who created the world. . . . In a world which desires unity and peace, but experiences a thousand tensions and conflicts, should not believers come together? Dialogue between Christians and Muslims is today more urgent than ever. It flows from fidelity to God. Too often in the past, we have opposed each other in polemics and wars. I believe that today God invites us to change old practices. We must respect each other and we must stimulate each other in good works on the path to righteousness.[10]

In 1986, John Paul II invited 108 leaders from all the major religions and many native and indigenous religious communities to Assisi, the home of St. Francis, for a "World Day of Prayer for Peace." The leaders present joined in prayer, meditation, and fasting as they committed themselves to work fervently for peace in a war-torn world. John Paul II was the first pope to visit a mosque—in Egypt and in Damascus. He was the first to visit a synagogue (in Rome) and to travel to Jerusalem to meet with Jewish and Christian and Muslim communities.

John Paul II's successor, Pope Benedict XVI, appeared not to make interfaith relationships as high a priority. His successor, however, Pope Francis, picked up where John Paul II left off. He took the name Francis to honor the man of peace who loved and sought to protect all of creation. As we noted in chapter 3, St. Francis challenged prevailing assumptions about Islam, and he modeled respectful dialogue and mutual witness by famously crossing battle lines in the midst of the Fifth Crusade.

From Institutional Dialogue to Inner Dialogue

As both the WCC and Vatican launched their respective programs, the need for clarity on both the structure and the anticipated goals soon became evident. Larger international meetings convened by both institutions produced positive results but also surfaced areas that needed a great deal more attention. While most Christians engaged in initial Christian-Muslim gatherings had high hopes for concrete ways to organize meaningful cooperation in particular settings, the expectations of many Muslims were quite different. The Muslims wanted first to talk about and seek resolution on what many in their communities saw as serious ethical and philosophical issues created by some Christian missionaries. For example, objections were raised to ways some medical, relief, and educational efforts were perceived as deceptive ways to proselytize Muslims. On the positive side, the gatherings served to develop relationships and trust in order for honest exchanges to take place as people listened and engaged one another empathetically.

In both the WCC and Vatican programs, the first experiments with Christian-Muslim (and Christian-Jewish, Christian-Buddhist, etc.) dialogue events surfaced the need for more organized dialogue internally among Christians. Disagreements and animated debates led the WCC to organize a nine-day meeting in Chiang Mai, Thailand, in the spring of 1977. Eighty-six leaders from various Christian communities heard presentations and discussed the most divisive and contentious issues: the relationship between dialogue, mission, and witness; the danger of syncretism; and the theological significance of non-Christian religions. The gathering produced a substantial document, "Dialogue in Community." The text addresses the thorny issues and concludes that open dialogical encounter is not inhibited by the considerable diversity among Christians on dialogue, mission, and theological perspectives. Chiang Mai was followed two years later when 67 leaders from 30 countries joined 27 Kenyans and WCC staff for a weeklong conference on "Christian Presence and Witness in Relation to Muslim Neighbors." While a consensus on all issues was not achieved, the participants agreed on the necessity of mutuality in relationships. Essentially, the centrality of sharing the good news of the gospel must be accompanied by an appreciation for the missionary imperative that Muslims also share. Mutual understanding and respect are required.

The Vatican also convened Christian-Muslim and other interfaith dialogue events. While remaining internal debates paralleled those prominent in WCC-related Protestant and Orthodox leaders, the documents of Vatican II and the leadership of Pope Paul VI and later John Paul II provided a firm foundation. The pontiffs issued encyclicals and gave speeches; the Secretariat produced a bulletin to disseminate information on its work. Another Catholic institution based in Rome, Pontifico Istituto di Studi Arabi e d'islamistica, began in 1975 to produce scholarly works in an annual journal, *Islamochristiana*. In 1977, this Pontifical Institute started publishing a more popular quarterly journal for wider distribution in bishoprics and parishes: *Encounter—Documents for Muslim-Christian Understanding*.

Two decades after the creation of the Secretariat for Non-Christian Religions, Pope John Paul II endorsed and issued a statement prepared by twenty bishops working through the Secretariat. The document maintains the integrity of both mission and dialogue and makes explicit their intrinsic relationship:

> Mission is already constituted by the simple presence and living witness of the Christian life. . . . There is also the concrete commitment to the service of mankind and of all forms of activity for social development and for the struggle against poverty and structures which produce it. . . . There is as well the dialogue in which Christians meet the followers of other religious traditions in order to walk together towards the truth and work together in projects of common concern. . . . The totality of mission embraces all these elements.[11]

The emphasis on education about Islam and guidance from Rome on how to pursue dialogue throughout the Catholic Church helped to clarify six different types of dialogue. A brief review of these options and the interplay between them leads to a broader understanding of what interfaith dialogue is and how it relates to people of faith individually and in congregations today.

Parliamentary dialogue refers to the large assemblies convened for interfaith discussion. The 1893 World Parliament of Religions in Chicago was the earliest example. Other international organizations—the World Congress of Faiths (1936) and the World Conference on Religion and Peace (1990)—were inspired by the 1893 Parliament. In 1993, a second World Parliament was convened and a new organization formed to continue such conventions approximately every five years. These large international and multireligious gatherings tend to have a broad agenda aimed at fostering better cooperation among religious groups, seeking common ground on the challenges of peace, the environment, and so forth.[12]

Institutional dialogue is identified by organized efforts to initiate and facilitate various kinds of intentional dialogue gatherings. This best describes the initial focus of the WCC and Vatican

programs discussed above. After organizing international dialogue meetings at the outset, both of these global religious institutions focused a great deal of energy in facilitating institutional
dialogue programs through regional, national, and state councils
of churches and Catholic bishoprics, respectively. Many of the
ecumenically active U.S. Protestant denominations also initiated
dialogue programs as well. Christian-Muslim dialogue programs
have been one of the components at all levels of church organization since the 1980s.

Institutional dialogue gave rise to two other types of interfaith
dialogue: theological dialogue and spiritual dialogue. Theological dialogue among Christians and Muslims, for example, could
include exploration of commonalities and differences on issues
like the nature of God, understandings of God's revelation,
human responsibility toward creation, the understandings about
Jesus and what the Qur'an means by calling him a Messiah, and
so on. Theological dialogue may also include discussion about
the meaning of one's religion in the presence of religious pluralism. While such discussions would be threatening or even heretical to some in both religions, for others theological dialogue can
be highly informative and encouraging. The latter is particularly
true for Muslims who discover that many Christians embrace an
inclusive theology (the official position of the Roman Catholic
Church since Vatican II) or a pluralist/universalist theology and
for Christians who discover how many Muslims affirm the validity of a path to heaven for followers of Jesus.

Spiritual dialogue concentrates on deepening the spiritual life
through interfaith encounter. Rather than wrestle overtly with
theological differences, this form of interfaith dialogue seeks to
expand and nourish the spiritual dimension of life. The most
nonthreatening approach might include observing the worship of
others or hearing and sharing views on the meaning of prayer for
Muslims and Christians. In many settings, people from different
traditions have come together to pray for peace in their communities in services that mirror John Paul II's interfaith gathering
at Assisi in 1986. Some participants have gone much farther and
participated in joint worship experiences. Some organizations

like the World Conference on Religion and Peace include multireligious services as part of their conferences. Christian monks and nuns have also been at the forefront of spiritual dialogue, particularly in relationships with Muslims, Hindus, Buddhists, and others who self-identify as following a mystical path. In my experience, experiments that involve crossing over into the experiential realm are far more challenging to many than dialogue aimed at understanding and respectful cooperation.

A primary goal of institutional dialogue is to encourage what the WCC calls "Dialogue in Community" and the Vatican labels "Dialogue of Life." These are inclusive categories that encompass the unstructured interaction between people that can occur in everyday life, through common efforts on community or humanitarian projects, and at times of religious festivals or holy days. Intentional efforts to engage others across religious lines are sometimes led by worshiping communities but often pursued by individuals. We will expand on this form of interfaith engagement in the final chapter since it applies most directly to the specific things that people of faith can pursue in their home communities.

Finally, all of these types of dialogue should foster an "inner dialogue," an introspective process that is stimulated by interfaith encounters. What does one think when listening to the Muslim call to prayer or sharing in a meal to break the fast of Ramadan? In what ways are individuals attracted to or put off by reading the Qur'an or hearing a Muslim explaining what a passage means to them? How does interfaith encounter impact or change the inner landscape of an individual person of faith living in a religiously diverse community and world? A prominent twentieth-century example of inner dialogue resulting in life-changing action can be seen in the lives of Mahatma Gandhi and Martin Luther King Jr. Gandhi, a Hindu, was profoundly inspired by the teachings of Jesus in the Sermon on the Mount (Matthew 5–7). Martin Luther King Jr. was inspired in turn by the ways Gandhi put the teachings of Jesus into nonviolent actions to confront injustices and work to change the status quo in his society. Inner dialogue happens consciously and unconsciously through all types of interfaith encounters.

Insights Gained through Christian-Muslim Dialogue

The intentional efforts to develop programs for education and Christian-Muslim dialogical encounter produced substantial insights during and after the several decades highlighted above. We conclude this chapter by identifying five primary discoveries.

First, the impulses and convictions that spurred the Vatican and WCC to launch these efforts have not only stood the test of time; their value is also increasingly clear in the interdependent, religiously diverse, and far too quarrelsome world today. The need for respectful understanding and cooperation across religious lines has never been more important. The interfaith dialogue programs not only recognized the pragmatic needs; they also perceived that commitment as followers of Jesus requires these new initiatives. The respective programs learned through experiments and experience what worked best. They also discovered how much work was needed to address deeply held concerns among both their Muslim partners as well as many Christians in their communities.

Second, meaningful dialogue needs to address fundamental issues directly. Looking only for the least common denominator may avoid unpleasant points of disagreement, but it cannot provide the foundation for mutual respect, which is needed. Authentic dialogue requires honest discussion—both within one's own Christian community and with Muslim dialogue partners—of things that matter most. Leaders in both the WCC and the Vatican were wise to concentrate considerable attention on internal differences on vital issues like the relationship between mission and dialogue and the strikingly divergent theological views on particularity and pluralism. While no clear consensus has been reached among all Christians, the processes have resulted in widespread affirmations about the necessity for dialogue and its intrinsic connection to Christian mission today.

Third, the importance of careful planning and a focused agenda became clear rather quickly. A Christian-Muslim gathering could easily devolve into heated debates about important issues like the ongoing Arab-Israeli conflict. Determining the focus for the gathering was essential. One of the almost unavoidable flaws in the early initiatives was the fact that the Christian groups were organizing the events. Over time, it became important that there be cooperation and mutuality in planning and setting the agendas for Christian-Muslim dialogue. As more Muslim leaders became involved directly, the opportunities for joint planning increased.

A fourth insight or discovery resulting from organized institutional dialogue was their value for Muslim-Muslim dialogue. Whatever document a given Christian-Muslim dialogue program might produce—with points of agreement and points in need of additional discussion—the actual meeting was discovered to be invaluable. Whereas most Christians in the world are connected to larger institutional organizations like the Vatican, the WCC, regional ecumenical bodies, and denominational structures, there are not comparable counterparts among Muslims. There are many respected Sunni and Shi'ite religious leaders and some who lead smaller sectarian groups within Islam, but nothing akin to the structures within Christianity that bring people together regularly. Muslim participants soon recognized and appreciated how organized dialogue meetings provided a useful vehicle for Muslims to engage other Muslims. The conferences were important in their own right, to be sure, but much of what was most valuable took place over coffee, during meals and informal conversations around the edges of formal meetings and presentations. This same dynamic occurred in regional and local settings as well. Organized Christian-Muslim events provided an opportunity for internal dialogue among Muslims and Christians even as it nurtured friendships and helped develop trust both within and across religious lines.

The fifth insight comes from the efforts to broaden and deepen Christian-Muslim dialogue at all levels. The formal dialogue programs began as top-down initiatives, with church leaders seeking partners and developing programs that were global or regional in scope. Remarkable documents were produced and disseminated, but far too few people at the local level were initially aware of or engaged intentionally in Christian-Muslim dialogues. As Christian leaders encouraged their Muslim partners to be agents of education and initiators of interfaith understanding when they returned to their respective communities, these same Christians began to take steps to move this whole enterprise down to the local level, where dialogue in community and the dialogue of life could and should be nurtured and encouraged.

Questions for Discussion

1. How would you describe the ways mission, evangelism, and bearing witness are interrelated and also distinctive?
2. How can Christians bear witness to their faith in ways that respect the beliefs of others? What do you consider the primary barriers to respectful engagement across religious lines?
3. Prior to reading this chapter, how would you have described the Roman Catholic Church's official position on interfaith relations since Vatican II? How much have you heard about or been engaged with interfaith dialogue initiatives promoted by ecumenical organizations and/or programs within Protestant denominations? Where did you first learn of interfaith dialogue and cooperation initiatives? If these efforts have not been visible in your experience, what do you suppose accounts for this?
4. Many Christians find it easier to engage in dialogue and shared ministry with their Muslim neighbors if they can do so with other Christian groups. What opportunities like this are already happening in your community?
5. This chapter talks about the value of "inner dialogue," when Christians examine their own thoughts about Islam. If you were to have such a conversation with yourself, what questions would you ask?

Chapter Six

Peaceful Coexistence and Cooperation in a Dangerous World

Living into a Healthy and Hopeful Future

> For each among you We have appointed a law and a way.
> If God had so willed, He would have created you as one
> community, but [He has not done so] that He may test you
> in what He has given you; so compete with one another in
> good works. To God you shall all return, and He will tell
> you the truth about that which you are disputing.
>
> Qur'an 5:48, auth. trans.

The previous chapters presented a foundational understanding of Muslims' orientation to God and the world followed by an overview of the history of Christian-Muslim relationships. This backdrop enables us to comprehend more accurately some of the confusing religious and political dynamics today. The preceding chapter outlined how major changes among Western Christians—especially since the 1950s—have shaped both attitudes and approaches to interfaith engagement with Muslims. All of the above makes clear that neither community of believers is monolithic. On the contrary, sincere people of faith within both Christianity and Islam can be placed all across the theological and ideological spectrum. While there is no reason to assume that adherents in either religion will come to theological consensus on issues of particularity and pluralism, they should be able to agree on this: People of faith and goodwill must earnestly seek tangible

ways to enhance peaceful coexistence and constructive cooperation—locally, nationally, and internationally—in the dangerous
world of the twenty-first century.

Two of the questions most frequently posed when I speak
about Islam and the need for healthy Christian-Muslim relations
in churches are the following: "I'm only one person; what can I
do?" and "The issues are overwhelming; what difference can one
congregation make?" My response is always that we, as individuals and as communities of faith, can do a great deal to manifest
the love of God and love of neighbor in our setting. What we do
may not change the international dynamics markedly, but it can
make a great deal of difference in our communities. The call for
people of hope and goodwill is not so much to be successful as it
is to be faithful. In addition to what we might learn as individuals
and congregations who live and work in the midst of religious
pluralism, it is important to remember that we all have constitu-
encies. We have family members, friends, coworkers, and many
others with whom we have relationships and often influence. Visibly pursuing a fair-minded understanding of Islam in ways that
challenge the stereotypes and the forces fueling Islamophobia
may well have constructive ramifications in ways we may or may
not be able to observe.

The wise words from the Qur'an at the beginning of this chapter offer a valuable way to proceed. Recognizing both commonalities and differences, Christians should not be inhibited from
discussing and debating matters of greatest importance. But let
us now compete with one another in good works and trust that
God will ultimately sort out the truth about areas of dispute and
disagreement. How best can Christians live into a more hopeful
and healthy future? The way forward involves education, dialogical engagement, and tangible cooperation for the betterment of
our communities and society.

Education, Education, Education

Education is an ongoing process that involves not only learning new information but also unlearning some of what we think

we already know. In my experiences over four decades, many if not most non-Muslim Americans have a good deal of unlearning to do when it comes to Islam. Widespread Islamophobia in the West has been fueled by a long history of bias and negative stereotyping of Muslims, then reinforced by the deplorable actions of extremists in recent decades. The first requirement therefore must be a fair-minded approach to Islam. Every effort should be made to present information about Islam and Muslims that most Muslims can readily identify as accurate. The following example illustrates the point.

Imagine yourself as a Muslim living in Pakistan or Bangladesh. Your knowledge about Christians and Christianity is limited. It has been shaped by some awareness of passages in the Qur'an—though you are not a scholar or diligent student of the Qur'an and Hadith—and a view of history that includes the Crusades and more recent Western colonial domination of your country. In recent years, you have seen repeated media coverage of very disturbing actions directed at Muslims by Western (you assume Christian) leaders. You want to know more and decide to attend a five-week series of presentations about Christianity in your mosque. Hold that image, come back to where you are, and ask, "What would I hope the person(s) leading that five-week study of Christianity would present to their Muslim audience?" You would hope that they would provide an understanding of Christianity that most Christians could endorse as broadly accurate. You would hope that the teachers would not simply focus on the many manifestations of extremism to reinforce the worst stereotypes: pictures of dehumanizing torture of Muslims in Abu Ghraib prison in Iraq, the desecration of Qur'ans by burning or flushing down the toilet at the Guantanamo detention facility, demeaning portrayals of the prophet Muhammad in Western media, stories about prominent political and religious leaders calling Islam evil, or the oft-callous attitude displayed toward desperate Muslim refugees escaping wars in Syria and other countries. Although these and other deeply disturbing events are real, very few Christians would consider these to be central features of what it means for them to be followers of Jesus.

Fair-minded education should initially be as free as possible from value judgments. Value judgments are obviously important. But they should be based on an accurate understanding, not on simplistic stereotypes and highly distorted images of Islam and Muslims. Apply the Golden Rule: Seek first to understand Islam as you would like your religion to be understood by others.

Fortunately, there are many ways for individuals and groups to pursue educational opportunities about Islam. The primary target audiences for this book are individuals and congregations who seek to overcome fear and misinformation with an accurate overview of the world's second-largest religion. Having spoken in several hundred churches (and mosques and synagogues) for four decades, I know firsthand the widespread desire to break through stereotypes and look for positive ways to connect with Muslims in local communities. This book is presented as an educational resource for clergy, lay Christians, Muslims, concerned people of goodwill, and congregations to those ends.

Many colleges and universities now regularly offer semester-long courses that local citizens can audit. Many also offer short courses on Islam through a variety of lifelong learning programs. There are valuable and readily accessible audio and DVD lecture resources through popular and widely accessible programs like The Great Courses.[1] A wealth of information is readily accessible online through the website of The Pluralism Project. Since 1991, Harvard professor Diana Eck has headed a team of more than a hundred researchers who collect data and post resources along with up-to-date demographic information about America's religious diversity.[2]

In the years since the attacks of September 11, 2001, many churches have pursued one or more serious study programs for adults. Some occur during several consecutive adult study classes on Sunday mornings; some have devoted weekends for seminars; many have a special ninety-minute to two-hour program at a designated time and invite other churches to join in an ecumenical gathering focused on a more accurate understanding of Islam in their communities and in the world today. I have participated in scores of each of these types of educational programs over the years. There are many good options for fair-minded educational programs in churches and with other groups.

Some of the more conservative churches and denominational colleges where I've spoken have been most open initially to having someone from within the Christian community lead the study of Islam. Most, however, are happy to have local Muslims lead or participate in study programs. This is the approach many have found most valuable in over one hundred programs that I have done with the Imam of the largest mosque in Oklahoma during the past decade. Dr. Imad Enchassi and I have spoken together and engaged in lengthy times of question-and-answer discussions in churches, synagogues, mosques, universities, and junior colleges, and at alumni association events, Rotary clubs, and so on. In addition to providing information and speaking directly to whatever questions people wish to ask, such programs have a powerful impact in other ways. Hearing directly from an established and thoughtful American Muslim leader puts a human face on Islam that is so often missing. Humanizing the "other" is a major step in breaking through stereotypes that perpetuate generic fear about Muslims. And hundreds of people have made a point of saying that how Dr. Enchassi and I interact—where we agree and sometimes articulate different responses—models respectful relationships and friendships across religious lines. With a little effort, people in or near cities of 75,000 or more can find American Muslims to come and speak to their church or group. Muslim lay and religious leaders normally welcome the opportunity to talk about Islam and respond to questions. The challenge tends to be the coordination of schedules and not locating appropriate speakers.

In addition to learning about Islam, such educational programs can be highly informative as people learn more about the Muslims and their many contributions within the local community. The experience in my home state of Oklahoma is again instructive. Muslims comprise less than 1 percent of the population in the state, but they are disproportionately represented in many professions. Approximately 500 Muslims are practicing medical doctors in each of the state's two largest cities, Oklahoma City and Tulsa.

These numbers are generally in line with national estimates that 10–13 percent of physicians are Muslims while Muslims make up less than 5 percent of the U.S. population.[3] Both of the state's tier-one research universities—the University of Oklahoma and Oklahoma State University—have 40–50 tenured or tenure-track Muslims on their faculties. These numbers represent well over 5 percent of the total permanent faculty. The largest home builders in Oklahoma are two Iranian American brothers who first came to the University of Oklahoma to study architecture before the Iranian Revolution in 1979. They are known and appreciated throughout the state for their generous support of all kinds of charitable and humanitarian causes. Time and again when such basic demographic information is presented, the response of many non-Muslims is twofold. After saying, "I had no idea . . . ," people often pause, reflect, and then start speaking about the delightful man, Muhammad, who is their pharmacist or the gifted Muslim cardiologist who treated their parent.

In Oklahoma City, Muslims have created and supported a wide variety of important institutions, including Mercy Homeless Center, Muslims4Mercy (delivering meals), Mercy Youth Center, Mercy Mission (a clinic and home for abused women), and Mercy School—a private educational institution comparable to a Catholic School for middle and senior-high students. Each institution bears the name "Mercy" for a reason. Imam Enchassi, who grew up in a Palestinian refugee camp in Beirut, Lebanon, attended a Christian school. The influential teacher who loved and encouraged him was a Catholic nun named Miss Rahma. As a teenage boy, Enchassi hid in a chimney for more than 24 hours on September 16 and 17, 1982, while Lebanese Christian militia systematically killed over 1,500 people in his refugee camps of Sabra and Shatilla. When he emerged, he saw where the soldiers had used the blood of their victims to paint red crosses on doors of the slain. In his youth, he saw both the love of Jesus manifest through people like Miss Rahma and a horrific violence perpetrated by people in the name of Christ. He was convinced that Miss Rahma was the model for a follower of Jesus. In Arabic, *rahma* means "mercy." Each of the Islamic social service institutions in Oklahoma City is named in honor of the Lebanese Christian nun and her enduring example of what it means to love God and love one's neighbor.

Presentations with opportunities for questions and discussion also reveal a wide variety of ways many Muslims in North America and elsewhere have been speaking out against the violence and extremism getting most media attention. Efforts to issue statements, do television and radio interviews, and publish letters to the editor too often don't receive adequate attention. Imam Enchassi and others in his mosque sometimes stand at a busy intersection in northwest Oklahoma City and silently hold signs saying, "ISIS does not represent me!" In almost every program I've done with Imam Enchassi, one of the first questions someone will ask is a version of the following: "Islam is supposed to be a religion of peace, but where are the peaceful Muslims? Why haven't Muslims done more to speak out against violence and terrorism?" His response usually begins with a question: "Do you have access to Google? If so, you can discover many ways Muslims have been speaking out and releasing statements locally, nationally, and internationally."[4]

At this point it is useful to recall the striking international example of prominent Muslims taking initiative to speak out boldly for peace and cooperation that was cited in chapter 1. In the aftermath of a controversial speech in 2006 by then Pope Benedict XVI, 138 Muslim leaders released an open letter to the pontiff: "A Common Word between Us and You." The initiative was warmly welcomed and endorsed by many prominent Christians in the West. In the U.S. more than 300 Christian leaders signed an open letter in response and published it in the *New York Times* and other newspapers. In response, the number of Muslim signatories grew to over 300, while more than 450 Islamic organizations formally endorsed the statement.[5] While this project received a good deal of attention, I have found remarkably few people in churches who have any awareness of it.

Learning more about the work of Muslim institutions is another way to pursue a more accurate understanding of Islam today. Organizations like the Council on American-Islamic Relations (CAIR) and the Arab-American Anti-Discrimination

Committee (ADC) offer resources, present programs, and provide speakers in cities all over the country.[6] Again, the Internet enables access to resources much more readily than ever before. But, as with all things posted online, thoughtful assessment and, if needed, some guidance from Muslim friends or trusted sources can be helpful in determining the accuracy and value that Internet searches produce.

Among international Muslim organizations, the Aga Khan Foundation is one of the most remarkable yet often unknown among non-Muslims. Knowing something of the work of this Ismaili branch of Shiʻite Islam is eye-opening, particularly for non-Muslims who have largely viewed Islam as somehow inherently threatening or violent. Ismaili Muslims are the smaller of the two main branches of Shiʻites, with approximately 20 million adherents living in more than 25 countries. Their leader, the Aga Khan, is the 49th direct descendant of the prophet Muhammad. He assumed leadership of the community at age 20 in 1957. For more than sixty years, this soft-spoken man has dedicated his life and the considerable resources of the Foundation to bettering societies in many tangible ways, including development work in the poorest communities and constructive interfaith programs. The work is based on the firm conviction in the well-being and dignity of all human beings, regardless of faith, origin, or gender. In his many speeches and programmatic initiatives, the Aga Khan seeks to encourage and sustain healthy civil societies. Convinced that respectful pluralism is essential in defusing hatred and conflict, he and the Foundation emphasize enlightened education, moral, and material investments in support of our common humanity. With humility, the Aga Khan consistently urges (and supports) people to turn away from rigid dogma and approach others as human beings, without anger, without discrimination, and without preconceptions.[7]

In addition to resources available within the Roman Catholic Church, many Protestant denominations have programs and developed resources to facilitate interfaith education and cooperation among their churches. The American Baptists, Cooperative

Baptist Fellowship, and other Baptist groups, for example, convened a three-day national conference (January 9–11, 2009) for presentations and dialogue with eighty Baptist and Muslim leaders from around the United States. In the following decade, two more national Baptist-Muslim dialogue events have followed, with Baptists and the Islamic Society of North America planning the events together. Presbyterians, Lutherans, Methodists, Disciples of Christ, Episcopalians, and others have worked on Christian-Muslim relations in various ways in recent decades. Learning more about the different efforts and the resources available for churches is often an invaluable step in formulating plans at the local level.

Christian-Muslim Dialogue in Local Settings

The previous chapter detailed the origin of internationally organized initiatives for intentional Christian-Muslim dialogue. Both the WCC and the Vatican encouraged and promoted continuing efforts at all levels, from national ecumenical organizations and individual denominations to local churches. We now turn to specific options that local congregations and individuals can pursue as they continue an educational process while also nurturing relationships in their settings.

Given the wide range of possible topics, it is wise to plan for an organized Christian-Muslim dialogue thoughtfully. A good way to begin builds on the kinds of informational programs identified above. For many, initial conversations are often most productive when specific topics focus the discussions. Typical questions or topics might include the following:

- What are the primary requirements for the life of faith, and how are these made known?
- How do you pray as individuals and as a community?
- What are the most important religious holidays, and how are these celebrated or commemorated during a calendar year?

- How are the major life-cycle events—birth, coming of age, marriage, and death—acknowledged and formalized through rituals?
- How do you understand the role of prophets in God's revelation?
- How would you describe the different sects within your religion, and how would you define yourself within the diversity in your religion?
- For Muslims, it is often helpful to ask about their experiences and those of their children seeking to be faithful in a society that is not geared to accommodate their daily prayers, dietary restrictions, religious holidays, and so forth.

These kinds of questions are typically not threatening, but they can reveal a great deal quite quickly. As people define themselves, differences emerge: between first- and second-generation American Muslims; connections to the traditions of ancestral homelands; variations between Sunnis and Shi'ites; clarification about why some Muslim women wear contemporary Western attire while others prefer traditional clothing that covers their arms, legs, and hair; and many other differentiating factors surface. Monolithic images of the "other" fade quickly as human beings engage with other human beings who have families, hopes, dreams, and concerns that are universal.

Organized dialogues focused on these kinds of topics can work well with groups in churches or mosques. They can also be connected to meals. For more than fifteen years, Boston Avenue Methodist Church in downtown Tulsa initially hosted and now facilitates three events each year they call "Open Tables." The organizational planning committee includes representatives from the church, the Islamic Society of Tulsa, the Jewish Federation of Tulsa, the Hindu Temple of Greater Tulsa, and the Dialogue Institute. The purpose of Open Tables is to build relationships with and better understand persons of differing faiths through potluck-style dinners. Participants are asked to bring four things: a favorite dish to share, an open mind, respect for those of different traditions, and a readiness to dialogue. Participants report that open and honest discussion not only improves relationships with neighbors; it also often helps people to clarify their own values and beliefs. Many churches in different states have similar programs, some of which are focused on Jewish-Christian, Christian-Muslim, or Jewish-Christian-Muslim participation.

An increasingly popular and delightful variation is an interfaith Iftar, the evening meal that breaks the fast during the month of Ramadan. President and Mrs. Clinton hosted the first Ramadan Iftar in the White House in 1996, an annual tradition continued by presidents Bush and Obama. President Trump canceled the event in 2017 and in 2018 hosted an Iftar for Muslim diplomats, not American Muslim leaders as had been the practice. In communities across the land, Muslims invite Christians, Jews, and others to share a meal and participate in a program that explains the meaning of the fast for Muslims. During the past decade, I have attended three or four large gatherings (normally 200–500 people) at interfaith Iftars each year on four different university campuses, at events hosted by the governor, mayors, and Islamic organizations. At the University of Oklahoma, the Muslim Student Association organizes an event they call "Think Fast." They invite non-Muslim students, faculty, and staff to consider joining them in fasting on the day of the Iftar. They suggest that people who fast take the money they might have spent on food and donate it to a charity of their choice. Several hundred non-Muslims learn a great deal about Islam as their eyes are opened not only to the importance and meaning of this pillar of the faith but also to the diversity of Muslim students, faculty, and staff at the university. The interfaith Iftar movement continues to expand and now includes local mosques connecting with churches and synagogues in their communities, much like many Jewish communities (and families) have incorporated interfaith Seder meals into their traditional Passover events each year.[8]

Individuals have options and opportunities as well. The 2006 book *The Faith Club: A Muslim, a Christian, a Jew—Three Women Search for Understanding*[9] became a best seller and sparked a movement. The book records the story of three women who become friends and begin to meet regularly to discuss the similarities and differences in their religious traditions. Many people have been inspired by this model and pursued similar initiatives with different combinations of participants. More broadly, recall the Vatican and WCC's emphases on the "Dialogue of Life" and "Dialogue in Community," respectively. Both of these programs encourage individual Christians to be aware of the religious diversity in their communities and make intentional efforts to engage and befriend neighbors in the daily activities of life.

Working and Praying Together for the Betterment of the Community

Learning more about Islam through educational efforts and intentional dialogue initiatives does not imply agreement. Understanding traditional Muslim perspectives on Jesus as a great prophet but not divine is quite different from agreeing with that view. The divinity of Christ is one of those matters which the verse at the beginning of this chapter implies is disputed and will be clarified by God in the final analysis. Even so, disagreement on such fundamental matters of faith and doctrine does not preclude Christians and Muslims (and Jews as well) from working together for the betterment of society.

In fact, adherents in the Abrahamic religions and also others do work together every day on all kinds of issues and challenges facing the human community. It would never occur to research physicians—a Southern Baptist from South Carolina, a Jew from Boston, and a Muslim originally from India—working side by side at the Centers for Disease Control in Atlanta to say to one another, "I can't work with you on the problem of AIDS or combating the spread of the Ebola virus because we have different views on the divinity of Jesus." No, they are working on diseases that affect and threaten all people. We work together on common human problems—from the ecological crises to issues of global economic stability—all the time.

Increasingly, Christians, Muslims, Jews, and others have recognized the importance of intentional efforts to join together visibly in programs consistent with what their faith requires. A great example is seen with the building of homes for people in need through Habitat for Humanity. All across America, people in different religious congregations have joined together to work with Habitat to build homes for people in their community. Linking arms in such a way offers a rich opportunity to engage in the dialogue in life that increases understanding and nurtures friendships among neighbors.

Whenever congregations join together to build a Habitat house or share in an Iftar meal, participants should make every effort to draw media attention to the events. While the news media is always drawn to the most dramatic and sensational events, many local stations will also welcome positive stories from their communities. It thus is important, whenever possible, to widen the circle of awareness of constructive interfaith cooperation through media coverage, opinion articles, letters to the editor, stories in congregational newsletters, and so forth. Publicizing positive stories about Christian-Muslim cooperation not only helps counter the negative stereotypes about Islam; it also may inspire others. Individuals can also do simple things like sending e-mails with pictures attached to friends and family members as a way both to spread positive images of Christian-Muslim cooperation and, perhaps, help motivate others to make similar efforts.

For younger adults, the Interfaith Youth Core (IFYC) now offers a variety of excellent resources and well-designed programs focused particularly on developing interfaith cooperation on college campuses.[10] Eboo Patel, the founder of the Chicago-based nonprofit organization, is a Muslim American Rhodes Scholar. The IFYC continues to grow each year with conferences and online training programs, staff support, and grants to facilitate the efforts of students and faculty committed to interfaith understanding and cooperation.[11]

In many settings, chaplains from different religions have discovered the value of working together in the various settings where their ministries are being pursued: hospitals, prisons, and the military. I have been a consultant for and worked with groups of chaplains in these kinds of settings—as well as those who work with first responders like police and firefighters. It is often the case that these religious professionals are willing and eager to share information and learn from one another in order to be more effective in their respective ministries. In the area of prison ministries, for instance, many Christian chaplains have reported to me different ways they have benefited from the experiences and approaches of their Muslim counterparts as they labor to prepare prisoners for reentry into society and achieve lower rates of recidivism.

Interfaith prayer services are another meaningful way Christians, Muslims, and other people of faith have come together for the betterment of society. These gatherings are local versions of what Pope John Paul II modeled at the 1986 "World Day of Prayer for Peace" when he invited over a hundred representatives of different religious traditions for a day of prayer and fasting in Assisi. In many local settings, such interfaith prayer services have often been connected to traumatic international, national, or local events such as the terrorist attacks on September 11, 2001; the bombings at the Boston Marathon in 2013; or one of many horrific assaults and mass murders in schools or houses of worship during the past two decades. For many Christians, coming together with people of faith in other traditions to pray is extraordinarily meaningful. For some, any form of inclusive worship presents significant theological obstacles. We turn now to examine both obstacles and opportunities when Christian-Muslim dialogue and engagement moves beyond education, understanding, and cooperation.

A Deeper Level of Christian-Muslim Dialogue

As trust develops, Christian-Muslim dialogue can move to a deeper level, where more controversial issues are engaged. These may include areas of theological disagreement and varying political perspectives—the topics our parents warned us to avoid in polite company. But, as we have emphasized from the beginning, the stakes in the twenty-first century are far too high to risk continuing the history of misunderstanding and antipathy that has too often characterized Christian-Muslim relations.

It is important to recognize at the outset that Christians and Muslims have traditionally brought different assumptions to this level of dialogue. Chapters 2 and 3 above enable non-Muslims to have a better understanding of some key historical and political dynamics shaping the worldview of many Muslims today. Theological assumptions also begin at a different place. While both traditions affirm all human beings as children of God, the ways Christians and Muslims have broadly viewed the "other" was shaped by theology and history. From the outset, Muslims were not only aware of Jews and Christians as religious communities with distinctive doctrines and practices; they also knew that these religions had sacred texts. Islamic self-understanding builds on the validity of these religions as originally revealed through prophets.

A similar dynamic is evident in the recorded teachings of Jesus in the Gospels and among early believers. Jesus not only cites the authority of the Hebrew Bible that was known in his day— the Law and the Prophets—he is also portrayed as one who both reinterprets the law and fulfills the messianic promise. As most Christians interpreted the meaning of Jesus' death and resurrection, there was no obvious justification for a new prophetic religion to arise. Thus, the first Christians to encounter Muslims tended to view Islam as Muslims presented it: a new form of the same religion. Christians in Europe and the West, however, almost universally perceived Islam and issues of religious diversity—Jewish, pagan practices, and manifestations of Christianity decreed "heretical" by authorities—with animosity.

The Qur'an affirms religious diversity to be part of God's will for humankind. The passage above and others make it abundantly clear that God intentionally created religious diversity.[12] The Qur'an identifies numerous prophets but places particular emphasis on the revelations through Moses (the Torah) and Jesus (the Gospels). The text includes many positive affirmations for the "People of the Book," including the promise that Jews and Christians who have faith, trust in God and "the Last Day," and do what is righteous "shall have their reward" (Qur'an 2:62 and 5:69). The People of the Book are following true, revealed religions that, in spite of what Muslims believe are errors that have crept in, provide enough guidance that the followers of Moses and Jesus are able to achieve their heavenly reward.

At the same time, the Qur'an does not shy away from identifying key points of disagreement. Time and again, the People of the Book are urged to "come to a common word" on the radical understanding of monotheism and proper worship (e.g., 3:64; 4:171; 5:82; and 29:46). Christians are portrayed as in danger of compromising the unity of God with teachings about the divinity of Christ and the doctrine of the Trinity (e.g., 5:72–75; 5:117; and 112:3). Depending on where one placed the emphasis, Muslims were able to cite different passages in support of a positive approach to followers of Jesus or one that was more apprehensive because of the potentially grievous doctrinal errors. As with all religious traditions, historical and cultural contexts have substantially shaped understandings and practices. The impact of the Crusades and the influence of some polemical Muslim scholars[13] often tempered the most positive stance toward Christians. And clearly, some prominent extremists claiming inspiration from Islam today focus almost solely on a narrow interpretation that labels Jews, Christians, and most other Muslims as infidels who threaten their view of "true Islam."

Honest Christian-Muslim dialogue should engage what is most meaningful to each participant. Inevitably, the most substantial and critically important point of disagreement centers on the person of Jesus. In my experience, dialogue about the distinct differences between embracing Jesus as a great prophet and as the incarnation of God can be more productive and thought provoking than simply outlining positions and agreeing to disagree. An experience on the outskirts of Mecca in 1986 illuminates the point. I was serving as the Middle East Director for the National Council of Churches at that time. At the invitation of the President of the World Muslim League, the NCC General Secretary and I traveled with two other American church leaders for an official four-day visit to Saudi Arabia. On one evening, we were treated to a traditional bedouin feast just outside the precincts of Mecca. As Arabic coffee was served at the end of the meal, the host, a prominent sheikh, posed a question to Arie Brower, the NCC General Secretary: "Tell me, do you believe God has a son?" Reverend Brower figured where this might be going and immediately threw the question to me for a reply. My response began a fascinating discussion.

My first response was to repeat in Arabic the first half of the *shahadah*: "We believe there is no god but God." Mild laughter rippled through the assembled group as they knew what I'd done to affirm monotheism. The sheikh asked the question again, and I responded in the same way. When he asked a third time, I answered his question with other questions: "Let me ask you if you believe the Qur'an is the Word of God." When he said, "Of course!" I followed with another query: "Do you believe the Qur'an is perfect, eternal, and uncreated?" Again, he answered "Yes!" I then made this observation to start a deeper conversation:

> We both agree that there is only one God and God makes God's will known through revelation. We disagree on how God's revelation has come to us. You affirm God's revelation first and foremost in a book, the Qur'an. We Christians believe God's ultimate form of revelation has come in a person. We both call the revelation the "Word of God" and believe the "Word" to be eternal and uncreated. Muslims believe that Christians are in danger of compromising the Oneness of God because of the doctrine of the incarnation and the Trinity. But, I suggest, Muslims have a similar problem when you affirm the Qur'an to be the eternal, uncreated, and perfect "Word of God."

Gender roles and issues of human sexuality are also focal points that many on both sides will want to explore. Thoughtful and informed dialogue participants will likely discover how some stereotypical images don't hold up to scrutiny even as wide variations in theological perspectives and cultural traditions have and continue to influence ways adherents place themselves across a wide spectrum.

Comparing and reflecting on Christian and Islamic perspectives on human responsibility toward creation can be especially productive. Common moral and ethical religious bases may lead to effective interfaith advocacy to counter destructive human contributions to climate change and underscore our responsibility to future generations.

Dialogue on ultimate questions about afterlife can also be informative and provocative at the same time. Muslims, like Christians, are not of one mind on who gets into heaven and whether or not hell is an eternal place or an abode for purgation. Believers in both traditions hold to exclusivist, inclusivist, and pluralist (universalist) theological views when considering particularity and pluralism.

Truth over Fear: Love God and Love Your Neighbor

This study has addressed the widespread fear of Islam in the West by deconstructing monolithic images that portray the religion and Muslims as somehow inherently violent and menacing. Clarifying the basic worldview and meanings behind the ritual devotional duties that constitute the Five Pillars of Islam and engaging with Muslims directly makes clear the striking similarities linking Christians and Muslims as people of faith in the One God and as human beings who share many of the same hopes, dreams, and concerns.

There is one other significant source of fear that inhibits many Christians: the fear of theological relativism. The vigorous nineteenth- and twentieth-century debates among Christian missionaries and Christian leaders reflected in the preceding chapter centers on this understandable concern. And, while Christians almost certainly will remain far from united in their theological understanding of their faith in a religiously diverse world, loving God and loving one's neighbor and the Golden Rule are still the mandates for all who seek to follow Jesus. We conclude with reflections that may calm the concerns of those who hold fast to the most traditional forms of exclusivist theology.

I was serving as Youth Director at a Baptist church in Tulsa in the summer of 1971. The senior minister fit the image of a stereotypical Southern Baptist preacher/evangelist. He preached revivals, and every Sunday he would keep us singing a hymn of invitation until someone came forward to get saved or rededicate their life. As I was preparing to begin the Master of Divinity program at the Southern Baptist Theological Seminary in Louisville,

Kentucky, I asked him one day what he thought about the possibility of God's activity beyond the walls of the visible Christian community. His response was shocking. He said he was quite sure that God was doing all kinds of things in the world and that explicit faith in Christ was not the only means to salvation. He cited various biblical passages to illustrate that God's love extends to all creation. He focused on the story of Peter and Cornelius in the tenth chapter of Acts to illustrate how Peter was able to learn new things about God's work in the world that he had never imagined possible. When I asked him why he preached and evangelized the way he did, this was his response: "I know what Christ has done for me; my responsibility is to share that good news with others even though I'm 95 percent sure that all kinds of people are meaningfully related to God and that heaven will look much different than most of us imagine!" He went on to encourage my study of world religions without fear of discovering new truths. It was a wonderfully liberating moment.

For half a century since Vatican II, the official position of the Roman Catholic Church—by far the largest group of Christians—has been an inclusive theology. During that same fifty years, Christian theologians and clergy have written extensively and expounded continually on various ways to conceptualize the relationship between Christian faith and the world's other religious traditions. Today many Methodist, Presbyterian, Episcopalian, and other clergy are openly or quietly inclusivist or universalist in their understanding of particularity and pluralism. Periodically, highly visible previously exclusivist pastors like Carlton Pearson and Rob Bell engender vigorous responses when they begin preaching or writing books indicating their shift to a more inclusive or universalist theology.[14]

Some years ago *Christian Century* began a periodic and highly illuminating series in which clergy from different denominations candidly reveal "How I Changed My Mind." It is well worth remembering and thinking about important ways we all learn, unlearn, grow, and change over time. Whereas suicide was long believed to be a one-way ticket to hell, contemporary understandings about mental health and clinical depression have dramatically changed that theological perspective. Or, consider how many have reversed or revised traditional Christian approaches to slavery, women in ministry, and issues of human sexuality.

The Bible hasn't changed, but new ways of understanding and interpretation are possible as people of faith continue to live into their theology by incorporating new information and contemporary life experiences. Christians do not need to come to theological consensus in order to live out the commandments not to bear false witness against one's neighbor, to love God and love one's neighbor, and to live peaceably with everyone. In the end, we can trust God to sort out the truth about whatever things Christians, Muslims, and others have been disputing.

Questions for Discussion

1. If you were putting together an event about Islam for your small group or congregation, what information would you most want people to receive?
2. Imagine two lists: The first contains events that you know about where Muslims took actions critical of or harmful to others. The second contains the opposite: events you are familiar with where Muslims worked for the healing and betterment of their neighbors. Which list is longer, and why?
3. If you were to participate in a community Christian-Muslim dialogue, what are the first questions you would ask your Muslim neighbors? What would you most want Muslims to know about your faith perspective or what informs your worldview?
4. If you chose to move beyond dialogue into joint action, what kinds of projects can you see yourself pursuing?
5. This chapter identifies several types of Christian-Muslim programs or projects that have proven to be of great value. What other kinds of Christian-Muslim initiatives might be pursued in your view?

Notes

Introduction

1. Demographic information for many parts of the world is far from precise. It is clear that Christianity and Islam are the largest traditions, but these numbers broadly represent those who would identify themselves within these religions whether or not they are active and practicing adherents.

Chapter 1: The Peril and Promise of Interfaith Relations in the Twenty-First Century

1. See https://www.youtube.com/watch?v=DqrHQpRHwws.
2. See https://coldwarstudies.com/2010/06/07/the-nixon-approach-iran-and -iraq/.
3. Sayyid Qutb was not trained or educated as a scholar of Islam. His writings don't deal with the long history of theological discourse and varied traditions of Qur'anic exegesis or the centuries of nuanced reflections on Islamic jurisprudence. He simply argued that Islam provided a complete way of life and the Qur'an contains the guidance needed. His most influential books are *Social Justice in Islam* and *Milestones*. For an overview of the history of the Muslim Brotherhood, see Charles Kimball, "The Brotherhood," *Link*, April–May 2013, 3–13.
4. "Donald Trump Calls for Banning Muslims from Entering the U.S.," *New York Times*, December 7, 2015.
5. "Demonstrations in Streets, and at Airports, Protest Immigration Order," *New York Times*, January 29, 2017.
6. See www.theguardian.com, November 29, 2017.
7. "Mike Huckabee: Muslims Depart Mosques Like 'Uncorked Animals,' Throwing Rocks and Burning Cars," *Huffington Post*, August 8, 2013.

8. "After Nice, Gingrich Wants to 'Test' Every Muslim in the U.S. and Deport Sharia Believers," *Washington Post*, July 15, 2016.

9. "FOX News Host Jeanine Pirro Claims Ilhan Omar's Hijab Is 'Indicative of Her Adherence to Sharia Law," *Newsweek*, March 10, 2019. See www .newsweek.com/fox-news-jeanine-pirro-ilhan-omar-hijab-sharia-1357632.

10. "Roy Moore Thinks Muslims Shouldn't Be Allowed in Congress for a Reason That Doesn't Exist," www.newsweek.com, December 12, 2017.

11. "A New Low in Anti-Muslim Bias," www.cnn.com, September 19, 2014.

12. "Preacher's Anti-Islam Remarks Mobilize the White House," www.beliefnet .com.

13. The Rev. Jerry Vines at the Pastors' Conference prior to the Southern Baptist Convention meeting in St. Louis, June 10, 2002, reported by Robert Breed of the Associated Press.

14. In the aftermath of a mass shooting by a Muslim couple in San Bernardino, California, for example, Jerry Falwell Jr. urged students at Liberty University "to obtain guns so they could end those Muslims when they walked in." The packed auditorium at the convocation cheered with approval. See Eboo Patel, "How Jerry Falwell, Jr. is Spreading Islamophobia," *Chronicle of Higher Education*, December 11, 2015.

15. Rod Parsley, *Silent No More: Bringing Moral Clarity to America . . . While Freedom Still Rings* (Lake Mary, FL: Frontline, Charisma House, 2005).

16. "Muslim Leaders Assail Pope's Speech on Islam," *New York Times*, September 14, 2006.

17. See www.acommonword.com.

18. Wilfred Cantwell Smith, "Comparative Religion: Whither—and Why?," in *The History of Religions: Essays in Methodology*, ed. M. Eliade and J. M. Kitagawa (Chicago: University of Chicago Press, 1959), 34.

Chapter 2: The Five Pillars

1. There are several solid introductions to Islam. Two highly regarded general introduction textbooks are John Esposito, *Islam: The Straight Path*, 5th ed. (New York: Oxford University Press, 2016); and Frederick M. Denny, *An Introduction to Islam*, 4th ed. (Upper Saddle River, NJ: Pearson Prentice Hall, 2011). See also Tamara Sonn, *Islam: History, Religion, and Politics*, 3rd ed. (Malden, MA: Wiley-Blackwell, 2015), for a short but informative introduction.

2. The most comprehensive examination of the question "Do Muslims and Christians Worship the Same God?" is found in Miroslav Volf, *Allah: A Christian Response* (New York: HarperOne, 2011).

3. The classic overview of the Qur'anic passages about Jesus is found in Geoffrey Parrinder, *Jesus in the Qur'an*, reprint ed. (London: OneWorld Publishers, 2013). A more comprehensive examination that goes well beyond the Qur'an is found in Tarif Khalidi, *The Muslim Jesus: Sayings and Stories in Islamic Literature* (Cambridge, MA: Harvard University Press, 2001).

4. In addition to several books and online resources that detail components of the Hajj, an especially useful resource for non-Muslims is a 50-minute DVD produced in 2003 by National Geographic Society (Washington, DC) and titled *Inside Mecca*; available on YouTube.
5. The video *Inside Mecca* provides a rare look at every stage of the Hajj from the perspective of three pilgrims (from the U.S., South Africa, and Malaysia). For an elaboration on the rich symbolism and powerful connections that Muslims attach to the Hajj, see Robert Bianchi, *Guests of God: Pilgrimage and Politics in the Islamic World* (New York: Oxford University Press, 2004).
6. Traveling to Mecca at times other than the actual days designated for Hajj is called the Umrah, or "lesser pilgrimage." It is considered meritorious but not a substitute for Hajj. In the Shi'ite branches of Islam, there are many sacred places that pious believers venerate through pilgrimage.
7. Once I became more attentive, Jesus' practice and endorsement of fasting became obvious. After Jesus' baptism, Matthew and Luke report that Jesus fasted during 40 days in the desert as he prepared for his public ministry. In the Sermon on the Mount, Jesus instructs followers to fast in private and not visibly for public affirmation.
8. The phrase "and fasting" is found in the King James Version and many other translations but omitted in the New Revised Standard Version since it is not included in some of the most reliable ancient manuscripts.
9. See Barbara Brown Taylor, *Holy Envy: Finding God in the Faith of Others* (New York: HarperOne, 2019).

Chapter 3: Conflict and Cooperation

1. There are several reasons why the Middle East region has received a highly disproportionate amount of media coverage for several decades. First, Israel has been a key strategic political and military ally of the U.S. since its inception as a nation-state in 1948. Unlike any other place on earth, Israel/Palestine holds intensive religious importance with Jews and Christians. In addition, the world economic system was intimately connected with the vast, high-quality oil reserves in that region.
2. One of the most widely cited versions of the Constitution of Medina is found in Ibn Ishaq, *The Life of Muhammad (Sirat Rasul Allah)*, trans. A. Guillaume (Lahore, Pakistan: Oxford University Press, 1974), 231–33.
3. See Daniel J. Sahas, *John of Damascus on Islam* (Leiden: E. J. Brill, 1972).
4. For an intriguing if somewhat romanticized study of religious pluralism in Islamic Spain, see Maria Rosa Menocal, *The Ornament of the World: How Muslims, Jews, and Christians Created a Culture of Tolerance in Medieval Spain* (New York: Little, Brown & Co., 2002).
5. Ongoing tensions and disputes between Christian leaders in Rome and Constantinople reached the breaking point in 1054, when Pope Leo IX and Patriarch Michael Cerularius excommunicated one another. This marked

the definitive split between what would be the Roman Catholic Church and the Eastern Orthodox Churches. The mutual excommunications were only revoked in 1965 after a meeting between Pope Paul VI and Patriarch Athenagoras I in Jerusalem in 1964.

6. See Norman Daniel, *Islam and the West: The Making of an Image*, paperback reprint of the 1997 ed. (Oxford: OneWorld Publications, 2009); and Daniel, *The Arabs and Mediaeval Europe*, 2nd ed. (New York: Longman, 1979). A more accessible overview is found in a short series of lectures by another historian of the Middle Ages: R. W. Southern, *Western Views of Islam in the Middle Ages* (Cambridge, MA: Harvard University Press, 1978).

7. The descriptions of what Dante considered the crimes of Muhammad and Ali are found in Canto 28 of *The Inferno*.

8. Southern, *Western Views*, 67–109; Daniel, *Islam and the West*, 307.

9. Martin Luther, *On War against the Turks*, trans. C. M. Jacobs and R. C. Schultz, in *Luther's Works*, ed. H. T. Lehmann (Philadelphia: Fortress Press, 1967), 170–77.

10. See Thomas Jefferson, *The Jefferson Bible: The Life and Morals of Jesus of Nazareth*, Smithsonian ed. (Washington, DC: Smithsonian Books, 2011).

11. For a fascinating study of Jefferson and debates among founders, see Denise A. Spellberg, *Thomas Jefferson's Qur'an: Islam and the Founders* (New York: Alfred Knopf, 2013).

Chapter 4: The World We Actually Live In

1. Thomas Friedman, "The World We Actually Live In," *New York Times*, September 30, 2012.

2. Clifford Geertz, *Islam Observed*, paperback ed. (Chicago: University of Chicago Press, 1971).

3. Jeff Stein, "Can You Tell a Sunni from a Shi'ite?," *New York Times*, October 17, 2006.

4. For a comprehensive history of divisions and analysis of contemporary flashpoints, see Vali Nasr, *The Shia Revival: How Conflicts within Islam Will Shape the Future* (New York: W. W. Norton & Co., 2006).

5. For a gripping account and a cautionary tale of the overthrow of Iran's democratically elected government, see Stephen Kinzer, *All the Shah's Men: An American Coup and the Roots of Middle East Terror*, 2nd ed. (Hoboken, NJ: Wiley, 2008).

6. On the Southern Poverty Law Center, see www.splcenter.org.

7. A very helpful short introduction to Sharia is found in David Vishanoff, "Islamic Law: A Long Work in Progress" (*The Army Chaplaincy*, Winter–Spring 2009); available via https://david.vishanoff.com/long-work/. For comprehensive treatment, see John L. Esposito and Natana J. DeLong-Bas, *Sharia: What Everyone Needs to Know* (New York: Oxford University Press, 2018).

8. There are several helpful studies on Islam in America, including these: Jane I. Smith, *Islam in America*, 2nd ed. (New York: Columbia University Press, 2010); and Yvonne Y. Haddad and Jane I. Smith, eds., *The Oxford Handbook of American Islam* (New York: Oxford University Press, 2014).

Chapter 5: Faithful Response to Two Imperatives

1. Disciples of the Buddha (meaning the one who "woke up" or became enlightened) also carried his teachings out to others, inviting them to embrace the worldview and path he taught for some 45 years after his enlightenment. But Buddhists have traditionally not been as aggressive in pursuing missionary endeavors as have Christians and Muslims.

2. Many readers likely will be surprised to learn that it is also illegal for Christians and Muslims to proselytize in Israel today.

3. The Presbyterian mission in Iran was also organized into a synod until 1934, when it became independent on the 100-year anniversary of that missionary initiative. It is now The Evangelical Presbyterian Church of Iran.

4. For a detailed overview of the Christian churches and communities in the Middle East, see Charles Kimball, *Angle of Vision: Christians and the Middle East* (New York: Friendship Press, 1992).

5. I was involved in a striking example of the debates over mission and service in countries where it was illegal to proselytize. As a Baptist minister engaged in ecumenical work with Middle Eastern Christians, I was invited to Richmond, Virginia, by the head of the Foreign Mission Board of the Southern Baptist Convention to speak to their executive staff and trustees. They were locked in a debate about whether or not to continue support for a long-standing Baptist hospital in South Yemen. It was considered the best medical facility in that impoverished country. But the more fundamentalist trustees wanted to withdraw since the doctors and other missionaries there could not legally evangelize or start new churches. Drawing on my work with the MECC, the WCC, and NCCCUSA, I argued that there may be no more important form of Christian witness anywhere than what the Southern Baptists were doing in the name of Christ for the people in South Yemen. The majority agreed with the view that presence and witness is a powerful form of Christian mission, and the hospital remained open and fully supported for many more years.

6. Vatican II also formalized initiatives to pursue ecumenical relationships with organizations like the WCC and individual communions that had broken from the Roman Catholic Church nearly five centuries earlier, such as the Anglicans and Lutherans. One of the dramatic manifestations of this effort occurred on the 500th anniversary of Martin Luther's break with the Catholic Church. Pope Francis traveled to Sweden to join in the commemoration of the Protestant Reformation and publicly urged Catholics and Lutherans to forge greater unity.

7. *Nostra Aetate* (here sec. 2) and other documents from Vatican II are easily available online. For an excellent summary of the materials on interfaith relations, see "The Attitude of the Church toward the Followers of Other Religions (Reflections and Orientations on Dialogue and Mission)" (Vatican City: Secretariatus Pro Non Christianis, 1984); also online.

8. *Nostra Aetate*, sec. 3.

9. A helpful overview of the development of the officially sanctioned Catholic interfaith programs and documents in the first quarter century following Vatican II is available in John F. Hotchkin and John Borelli, "Roman Catholic Interreligious Offices and Documents," in *The Handbook for Interreligious Dialogue*, ed. John Borelli (Morristown, NJ: Silver, Burdett & Ginn, 1990), 51–56.

10. See Thomas Michel, "Pope John Paul II's Teaching about Islam in His Addresses to Muslims," *Bulletin: Secretriatus pro non Christianis* 21, no. 2 (1986): 10–11.

11. See "The Attitude of the Church toward the Followers of Other Religions (Reflections and Orientations on Dialogue and Mission)."

12. The histories, organizational structures, and programs of these groups can be easily located and explored online via their respective websites.

Chapter 6: Peaceful Coexistence and Cooperation in a Dangerous World

1. The Teaching Company (Chantilly, VA) has produced multiple courses on world religions by award-winning professors. The normal format is 24 lectures, each 30 minutes long. A good place to start is with my course Comparative Religion or John Esposito's Great World Religions: Islam. In addition to the tens of thousands of individuals who have purchased the course, I know of many churches that have used Comparative Religion for a two-semester study of world religions in adult education classes. These classes typically watch a 30-minute lecture and then have an additional half hour for discussion. For a list and description of all the courses provided by The Teaching Company, see www.thegreatcourses.com.

2. The URL for The Pluralism Project: pluralism.org.

3. Precise statistics are difficult to confirm, particularly since many Muslims and other minorities have been reluctant to include religious affiliation on official forms or census data.

4. Simply do an Internet search for "Muslims denouncing terrorism" or some such wording, and you will discover numerous articles and formal statements by thousands of Muslim leaders and communities, including several from international conferences organized specifically to address this issue directly.

5. For an overview of this Muslim initiative and the Christian responses, see John Esposito, *The Future of Islam* (New York: Oxford University Press, 2010), 187–90.

6. Information on these national organizations can be found at their respective websites: www.cair.com and www.adc.org.

7. The Aga Khan, *Where Hope Takes Root: Democracy and Pluralism in an Inter-dependent* World (Vancouver: Douglas & McIntyre, 2008), 4–6. This book is a highly instructive collection of the Aga Khan's speeches on "Enhancing Pluralism," "Underwriting Human Progress," "Democracy, Pluralism and Civil Society," "Pluralism Is a Work in Progress," and other topics relevant to our study.

8. At times, other events can be combined in especially meaningful ways. During Ramadan in 2018, for instance, the Muslim community in Stillwater, Oklahoma, hosted an interfaith Iftar on conjunction with the opening of their new mosque adjacent to the campus of Oklahoma State University. Muslims from around the state joined with many Christians invited for the event. The two speakers were a visiting Imam from Texas and the president of OSU. The Imam highlighted the meanings of the fast for Muslims while President Burns Hargis spoke eloquently about the importance of the new mosque and the positive interfaith relationships on the campus and in the community.

9. Ranya Idliby, Suzanne Oliver, and Priscilla Warner, *The Faith Club: A Muslim, a Christian, a Jew—Three Women Search for Understanding* (New York: Free Press, 2006; reprint, New York: Simon & Schuster, Atriya Books, 2007).

10. See Kathleen M. Goodman, Mary Ellen Giess, and Eboo Patel, eds., *Educating about Religious Diversity and Interfaith Engagement: A Handbook for Student Affairs* (Sterling, VA: Stylus Publications, 2019) for a helpful collection of pedagogical tools—programs, activities, events, and case studies—to facilitate constructive interfaith initiatives on college campuses.

11. Interfaith Youth Core website (www.ifyc.org) provides many details about their history, resources, and programs. See Eboo Patel's book *Acts of Faith: The Story of an American Muslim, the Struggle for the Soul of a Generation* (Boston: Beacon Press, 2007) for the remarkable life journey that led him to create the IFYC.

12. One of the most frequently cited of such passages is Qur'an 49:13: "O mankind! Truly We created you male and female, and We made you peoples and tribes that you may come to know one another. Surely the most noble of you before God is the most reverent of you. Truly God is Knowing, Aware."

13. Ibn Taymiya (d. 1328) was one of the most celebrated and influential Muslim scholars in the era of the Crusades. His book *The Correct Answer to Those Who Changed the Religion of Christ* catalogs the major theological and philosophical points of criticism directed at those who came after Jesus: altering the divine revelation, propagating errant doctrine, and dangerous mistakes in religious practices. For an abridgement in English, see https://ahlalhadeeth .files.wordpress.com/2012/06/answering_those_who_altered_the_religion_of _jesus_christ.pdf.

14. Carlton Pearson was senior pastor at the largest church in Tulsa, Oklahoma, and a member of the Board of Regents at his alma mater, Oral Roberts University, when he became convinced that God's love and gift of grace extended to all people. See Carlton Pearson, *The Gospel of Inclusion: Reaching beyond*

Fundamentalism to the True Love of God and Self (New York: Simon & Schuster, Atria Books, 2009); and National Public Radio's thisamericanlife.org ("Heretics" broadcast on December 16, 2005). Rob Bell, a popular evangelical pastor of a large church in Detroit, provoked a tremendous response—positive and negative—with the publication of his book *Love Wins: Heaven, Hell, and the Fate of Every Person Who Ever Lived* (San Francisco: HarperOne, 2009).

For Further Reading

Abdul Rauf, Feisal. *What's Right with Islam: A New Vision for Muslims and the West.* San Francisco: HarperSanFrancisco, 2004.

Aga Khan. *Where Hope Takes Root: Democracy and Pluralism in an Interdependent World.* Vancouver: Douglas & McIntyre, 2008.

Ahmed an-Nai'im, Abdullahi. *Islam and the Secular State: Negotiating the Future of Shari'a.* Cambridge, MA: Harvard University Press, 2008.

Ariarajah, S. Wesley. *Not without My Neighbor: Issues in Interfaith Relations.* Geneva: World Council of Churches, 1999.

———. *The Bible and People of Other Faiths.* Maryknoll, NY: Orbis Books, 1989.

Aslan, Reza. *No god but God: The Origins, Evolution, and Future of Islam.* New York: Random House, 2005.

Bianchi, Robert R. *Guests of God: Pilgrimage and Politics in the Islamic World.* New York: Oxford University Press, 2004.

Curtis, Edward E., IV. *The Columbia Sourcebook of Muslims in the United States.* New York: Columbia University Press, 2009.

Denny, Frederick M. *An Introduction to Islam.* 4th ed. Upper Saddle River, NJ: Pearson Prentice Hall, 2011.

Eck, Diana L. *A New Religious America: How a "Christian Country" Has Become the World's Most Religiously Diverse Nation.* San Francisco: HarperSanFrancisco, 2001.

———. *The Pluralism Project.* www.pluralism.org. Also, http://pluralism.org/ocg/. Cambridge, MA: Harvard University, 1991–.

Esposito, John L. *The Future of Islam.* New York: Oxford University Press, 2010.

———. *Islam: The Straight Path.* 5th ed. New York: Oxford University Press, 2016.

Esposito, John L., and Natana J. Delong-Bas. *Shariah: What Everyone Needs to Know.* New York: Oxford University Press, 2018.

Geertz, Clifford. *Islam Observed.* Chicago: University of Chicago Press, 1971.

Goodman, Kathleen M., Mary Ellen Giess, and Eboo Patel. *Educating about Religious Diversity and Interfaith Engagement: A Handbook for Student Affairs.* Sterling, VA: Stylus Publishing, 2019.

Gottschalk, Peter, and Gabriel Greenberg. *Islamophobia and Anti-Muslim Sentiment.* 2nd ed. Lanham, MD: Rowman & Littlefield, 2019.

Green, Todd H. *The Fear of Islam: An Introduction to Islamophobia in the West.* Minneapolis: Fortress Press, 2015.

———. *Presumed Guilty: Why We Shouldn't Ask Muslims to Condemn Terrorism.* Minneapolis: Fortress Press, 2018.

"Guidelines on Dialogue with People of Living Faiths and Ideologies." *International Bulletin of Mission Research* 4, no. 4 (October 1, 1979): 160–62. Reissued, Geneva: World Council of Churches, 2010. Available online by the title.

Haddad, Yvonne Y., and Jane I. Smith, eds. *The Oxford Handbook of American Islam.* New York: Oxford University Press, 2014.

Idliby, Ranya, Suzanne Oliver, and Priscilla Warner. *The Faith Club: A Muslim, a Christian, a Jew—Three Women Search for Understanding.* New York: Free Press, 2006. The website growing out of this publication: www:thefaithclub .com.

Inside Mecca. DVD produced by the National Geographic Society. Washington, DC: National Geographic Society, 2002.

Kazi, Nazia. *Islamophobia, Race, and Global Politics.* Lanham, MD: Rowman & Littlefield, 2019.

Khalidi, Tarif. *The Muslim Jesus: Sayings and Stories in Islamic Literature.* Cambridge, MA: Harvard University Press, 2001.

Kimball, Charles. *Comparative Religion.* Great Courses DVD of 24 lectures. Chantilly, VA: The Teaching Company, 2008.

———. *When Religion Becomes Evil: Five Warning Signs.* Revised and updated edition. New York: HarperOne, 2008.

———. *When Religion Becomes Lethal: The Volatile Mix of Politics and Religion in Judaism, Christianity, and Islam.* San Francisco: Jossey Bass, 2011.

Kinzer, Stephen. *All the Shah's Men: An American Coup and the Roots of Middle East Terror.* 2nd ed. Hoboken, NJ: Wiley, 2008.

Menocal, Maria Rosa. *The Ornament of the World: How Muslims, Jews, and Christians Created a Culture of Tolerance in Medieval Spain.* New York: Little, Brown & Co., 2002.

Nasr, Vali. *The Shia Revival: How Conflicts within Islam Will Shape the Future.* New York: W. W. Norton & Co., 2006.

National Council of Churches of Christ in the USA. "Getting to Know Neighbors of Other Faiths: A Theological Rationale for Interfaith Relationships." See http://nationalcouncilofchurches.us/shared-ministry/interfaith/neighbors3 .pdf.

———. "Interfaith Relations and the Church: Study Guides on Key Issues." See http://nationalcouncilofchurches.us/shared-ministry/interfaith/resources .php.

Olson, Richard P. *Side by Side: Being Christian in a Multifaith World.* Valley Forge, PA: Judson Press, 2018.

Patel, Eboo. *Acts of Faith: The Story of an American Muslim, the Struggle for the Soul of a Generation.* Boston: Beacon Press, 2007.

———. *Out of Many Faiths: Religious Diversity and the American Promise.* Our Compelling Interests 4. Princeton, NJ: Princeton University Press, 2018.

———. *Sacred Ground: Pluralism, Prejudice, and the Promise of America.* Boston: Beacon Press, 2012.

Ramadan, Tariq. *Western Muslims and the Future of Islam.* New York: Oxford University Press, 2004.

Sacks, Jonathan. *The Dignity of Difference: How to Avoid the Clash of Civilizations.* New York: Continuum, 2002.

Shenk, David W. *Christian, Muslim, Friend: Twelve Paths to Real Relationship.* Harrisonburg, VA: Herald Press, 2014.

Smith, Jane I. *Islam in America.* 2nd ed. New York: Columbia University Press, 2010.

Sonn, Tamara. *Islam: History, Religion, and Politics.* 3rd ed. Malden, MA: Wiley-Blackwell, 2015.

Taylor, Barbara Brown. *Holy Envy: Finding God in the Faith of Others.* New York: HarperOne, 2019.

Uddin, Asma T. *When Islam Is Not a Religion: Inside America's Fight for Religious Freedom.* New York: Pegasus Books, 2019.

Volf, Miroslav. *Allah: A Christian Response.* New York: HarperOne, 2011.

Wogaman, J. Philip. *What Christians Can Learn from Other Religions.* Louisville, KY: Westminster John Knox Press, 2014.

Zogby, James. *Arab Voices: What They Are Saying to Us and Why It Matters.* New York: Palgrave MacMillan, 2010.

Index

147

population of, 2
Qur'an on, 29–30
violent acts of, 2, 71, 117
Christianity/Judaism/Islam
comparisons
and charitable giving, 43
and fasting, 42–43
monotheism, 40
pilgrimages, 43–44
and prayer, 41–42
and revelations from God, 40–41
Christian-Muslim relations, future of
in communities, 123–25
and cooperation, for good, 126–28
and dialogue, meaningful, 128–32
education for (*See* education,
Westerners of Islam)
and inclusivism, 132–34
of individuals, 125–27
letters regarding peace 2006,
19–20, 121
church programs, on Islam, 118–19,
123–26
civilizational system, Muslim contributions to, 78
civilizations, clash of, 48
classes, on Islam, 118
colonialism, end of, 78–79
commandments, 23
"Common Word between Us and
You, A," 19–20, 121
communities, diverse
and charter of Medina, 52
Christians in Middle East, 28,
48–49, 98–99, 101–2
in eighth century CE, 56
in United States, 124–25
working together, 126–28
compassion, for fellow humans, 23,
94–95, 132–34
confession of faith, 27–32, 40
congregations, and dialogue events,
123–26

consensus, in Islamic Law, 84
Constitution of Medina, 52–53,
137n2
controversial issues, interfaith dialogue and, 128–29
conversion, to Islam, 56, 89, 96
cooperation, interfaith, 126–28
Coptic Orthodox churches, 100
Council on American Islamic Relations (CAIR), 121
Cragg, Kenneth, 66
Cribratio alchorani (Nicholas of
Cusa), 60
criminal codes, in Islamic Law,
84–85
Crusades, and Western views on
Islam, 57–61

Daniel, Norman, 57
Dante, 59
da'wah, 95
Day of Atonement, 42
"Declaration on the Relations of the
Church to Non-Christian Religions, The," 104
defamation, 23–24
deities, in sixth century CE, 49–50
De pace fidei (Nicholas of Cusa), 60
depictions of Muhammad, 58–59,
86–88
depression, 133–34
dervishes, whirling, 77
DFI (Dialogue with People of Living
Faiths and Ideologies), 103
dialogue, interfaith
of controversial issues, 128–32
and disagreements, 130
events, 107, 109, 112, 123–26
insights gained from, 111–13
types of (*See* dialogue types)
from the Vatican, 103–9
from the World Council of
Churches (WCC), 102–6

CPSIA information can be obtained
at www.ICGtesting.com
Printed in the USA
FSHW021253170320
68212FS

Smithsonian
THE MOON

by James Buckley Jr.

Penguin Young Readers
An Imprint of Penguin Random House

Contents

Look Up!

People have looked up at the
Moon for thousands and thousands
of years. No matter where you are
on Earth, you can see it. The Moon
travels around the Earth. Together,
the Earth and the Moon travel
around the Sun. The Moon is a part
of our sky and our lives.

Let's meet our closest neighbor
in space!

From the beginning, people wondered, "What is the Moon?" They answered that question with stories that have been handed down over many, many years.

In some American Indian stories, the Moon helped create the universe and life on Earth.

Long ago the Greeks, the Romans, and the Chinese honored a moon goddess.

The moon goddess Chang'e

Tlingit people of Alaska tell of a chief who held the Sun and the
oxes. Raven set them free. Then there was light, day, and night.

An English folktale says that the Moon is made of green cheese.

Have you heard of the "Man in the Moon"? There are many stories about this "face" on the Moon's surface.

The Moon has also inspired writers. The famous French author Jules Verne wrote *From the Earth to the Moon* in 1865. But by that time, we had learned many facts about the Moon.

Keeping Time

Early Moon watchers saw that the Moon appeared to rise and set. They also noticed that it appeared to change shape. People saw that these events happened in a **pattern**. The Moon changed the same way, time after time.

Since people long ago did not
have clocks, they **observed** the world
around them to keep track of time.
One of the best ways to keep time
was to watch the Moon.

The Moon takes about 29 days to go around the Earth once. Those 29 days came to be called a month.

People began to break up each year into how many times the Moon went through this pattern. The 12 times the Moon changed became the 12 months of the year.

A moon chart from 1708

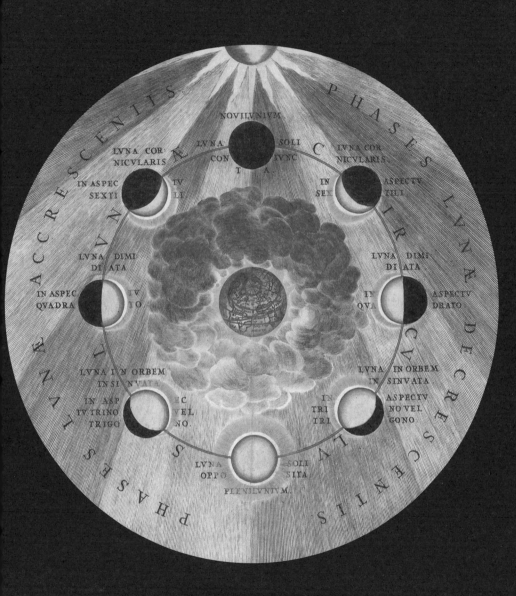

A Closer Look

How did people first look at the Moon? They used their eyes, of course!

But some people wanted a closer look, so in the 1600s, they developed telescopes. An Italian scientist of that time named Galileo Galilei built a telescope. He could see the Moon close-up with it.

The Moon had an uneven surface. Some areas were rough, and some were smooth. Galileo and other scientists began to study the Moon closely.

Galileo and his telescope

Over time, people built bigger and bigger telescopes. They spied huge craters, hills, and mountains on the Moon. But there was no "Man in the Moon." In fact, there were no signs of life.

Today, the most important telescope is not even on Earth. The Hubble Space Telescope orbits Earth like the Moon does. It has taken amazing photos of the Moon from space.

Not Cheese!

Looking through all those telescopes proved that the Moon isn't green or cheesy!

The Moon is really made from rock. Scientists say the Moon was formed more than 4 billion years ago.

An object as big as Mars smashed into the Earth. Pieces of this space object and the Earth broke off in the impact. This **debris** floated around the Earth. Over time, the pieces came together to form the Moon.

The Moon in Motion

The Moon's path around the Earth is called an **orbit**. The Moon also spins like a top as it orbits Earth. That's why we always see the same side of the Moon.

The near side of the Moon

The Moon takes about 29 days
to spin around once, the same as it
takes to orbit the Earth once.

The far side of the Moon

Why does the Moon change shape?

It doesn't!

What changes is how much of the Moon is hit by the Sun's light. The Moon does not make light. It shines by reflecting light from the Sun.

As the Moon orbits, a different part is lit each night. That's why it appears to change shape over a month.

This pattern is called the **phases** of the Moon.

Hide-and-Seek Moon

Sometimes, the Earth comes between the Sun and the Moon. Our planet blocks the Sun's light from hitting the Moon for a few minutes. This is called a **lunar** eclipse. **Lunar** means "having to do with the Moon."

Lunar eclipse

Other times, the Moon blocks the Sun's rays from the Earth. This is called a **solar** eclipse. **Solar** means "having to do with the Sun."

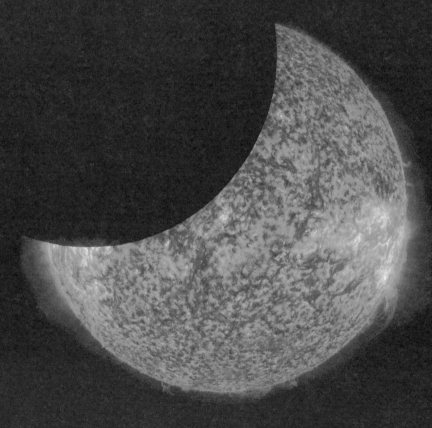

Solar eclipse

Tides

Gravity is the force that holds us on Earth. Gravity also keeps Earth in orbit around the Sun. It keeps the Moon spinning around Earth, too.

Gravity works both ways. **Gravitational** pull from the Moon reaches the Earth. The Moon's gravity creates a daily change in the world's oceans.

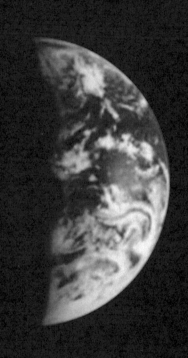

The Moon in orbit around Earth

The gravity of the Moon pulls
the oceans toward the Moon itself.
The water **bulges** toward the Moon.
As the Moon orbits, the bulge in the
oceans moves with it.

That movement is called the **tide**.
The tide comes in and out twice
a day where oceans meet land—
thanks to the Moon!

The Real Men on the Moon

Studying the Moon from afar was not enough. People wanted to *go* there.

In the 1950s, new rockets were built. Soon, the United States and the Soviet Union each launched people into space with these powerful machines.

Yuri Gagarin of the Soviet Union, the first human in space

In 1961, the president of the United States, John F. Kennedy, set a goal: reach the Moon itself by 1969. The space race was on!

President John F. Kennedy

In the early 1960s, the United States sent the Mercury **astronauts** into space. They orbited the Earth and learned about space travel.

The Mercury missions were practice for traveling to the Moon.

John Glenn squeezes into the Mercury Friendship 7 **capsule**. He became the first American to orbit the Earth.

A later space program was called Apollo, after the Greek god of the Sun. These spaceflights used even larger rockets. Some of them sent people into orbit around the Moon for the first time.

Each Apollo mission was given a number. During Apollo 8, the astronauts took some famous photos.

For the first time in human history, we were able to see what our planet looked like from the Moon!

Earth rise

Now it was time to win the space race! Apollo 11 launched on July 16, 1969. On board were astronauts Neil Armstrong, Edwin "Buzz" Aldrin, and Michael Collins.

It took Apollo 11 three days to reach the Moon. Armstrong and Aldrin landed a lunar craft on the Moon's surface. Collins stayed on board the spacecraft to pick up the other two.

Apollo 11 cuff links

Apollo 11 checklist

Apollo 11 patch

Blast off, Apollo 11

On July 20, Neil Armstrong became the first human to step onto the Moon. His words are famous: "One small step for a man, one giant leap for mankind."

Neil Armstrong

The flag and a TV camera

A bootprint that is still there!

Beyond Apollo 11

Apollo 11's crew were welcomed back to Earth as heroes.

Even though they had landed on the Moon, the Apollo space program continued. Apollo 12's astronauts dug up lunar soil. They gathered about 70 pounds of Moon rocks. Scientists on Earth studied what they brought back.

Lunar soil sample

Apollo 13's astronauts didn't make it to the Moon. They almost didn't make it back to Earth!

A dangerous problem arose on the moving spacecraft. The Apollo crew and mission control on Earth had a tense few days to deal with. The astronauts barely returned safely.

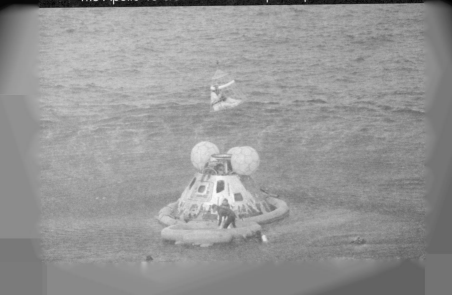

The Apollo 13 crew after their capsule splashed down

The troubles with Apollo 13 didn't stop the space program, though. On the next mission, Apollo 14 astronaut Alan Shepard brought a golf club with him. He hit the first golf ball on the Moon!

Alan Shepard

Astronauts on Apollo 15 didn't just walk on the Moon—they drove! A special **lunar rover** was built to help them explore larger areas. Crews on Apollo 16 and 17 used the rover as well.

Apollo 17 was the last time that human beings visited the Moon . . . so far!

The lunar rover, Apollo 17

People are still exploring the Moon with spacecraft. These **robotic** spacecraft circle the Moon and take photographs. Scientists are even discussing building bases on the Moon.

Our Moon is not the only moon in the solar system. Scientists have counted 145 moons around the eight planets.

Could there be other life in the universe? Do you think they look up at their own moons like we do?

Artwork of some moons in our solar system

Glossary

astronaut: a person who travels to space

bulges: expands and changes shape

capsule: the part of a rocket that carries the astronauts

debris: broken parts of a whole

gravitational: having to do with gravity, the force that holds

objects to Earth or other bodies in space

lunar: having to do with the Moon

lunar rover: a four-wheel electric vehicle driven on the Moon

observed: looked at over time

orbit: the path of one object in space around another

pattern: something that repeats in an order

phases: the different ways that the Moon appears to people

on Earth as a month goes by

robotic: having to do with robots; powered by robot technology

solar: having to do with the Sun or sunlight

tide: the twice-daily flow of ocean water toward and away

from a shore